To Aunt Janett
You've been like
Without a doubt you ''
of the most influential perso''
my life. I Thank God For you Al''

Love
Will L. Broug
3-17-21

AND
STILL CHAMPION

Compiled by Prince Blair

Edited by Christine Bode

Book Cover Design by Trevor Bailey

Book Production by Dawn James, Publish and Promote

Design and Layout by Davor Nikolic

Printed and bound in the United States of America.

Note to the reader:
The events in this book are based on the writers' memories from their perspective. Certain names have been changed to protect the identity of those mentioned. The information is provided for educational purposes only. In the event you use any of the information in this book for yourself, which is your constitutional right, the author and publisher assume no responsibility for your actions.

DEDICATION

And Still Champion

I dedicate this book to my beautiful and loving wife Michelle who without question is my better half. You have been the wind beneath my wings. Thank you for your prayers, love, and support through this journey.

To

my son Prince Jr. (PJ),

my nephew Tommy (Rock),

and my grandson Damon.

I pray that each of you finds the Champion within and know that with God all things are possible.

I would like to thank each author for their commitment and contribution.

Finally,

I dedicate this book and my life to God, my Heavenly Father.

TABLE OF CONTENTS

FOREWORD

'And Still Champion'

Black men in every walk of life encounter a confluence of being stigmatized, dismissed, feared, hated, undervalued, and targeted as enemies of the state. The mind, body, and soul of Black men are collectively at risk, as the struggle for mere survival is readily present in their daily lives. The mental gymnastics required to diminish the threat of death, ridicule, and psychological assault is wearying. Yet with these seemingly insurmountable odds, there is an expectation to lead, provide, and flourish while existing with their backs up against the wall.

White supremacy culture, the progenitor of slavery and racism, constructed a false narrative that Black men are beasts, void of complete humanity that demands emotional, relational, and spiritual support to thrive. We must buy out of these myths en route to a more credible representation of Black manhood if our full humanity is to be recognized en masse.

Landing in Queens, New York, in the fall of 1996, I was fixed on pursuing an acting career in the big city. A year out of college and a short stint in my hometown of Baltimore, I felt the momentum of booking numerous theater gigs and my first guest-starring role on NBC's *Homicide: Life on the Street.*

I had expectations of catching my big break as soon as the business caught wind of my emerging talent. But shortly after my arrival, I found myself wrestling with past demons and the new responsibility of caring for my great aunt, who was an amputee. I fell into a deep depression. Searching for ways to build community and compensate for my brokenness, I found my way to the Greater Allen A.M.E. Cathedral of New York. It was there I would have my first encounter with Prince Blair, the visionary and conduit for this work. Prince was a military veteran who recently made an about-face from street life, for which he was the major general, always at arms. He invited me to join him as a mentor for young Black boys in the Rites of Passage program, a ministry he recently came to lead. It was there I would discover my new tribe. I witnessed Prince's conviction to advocate, empower, and guide these young men in a direction far removed from the dark world he knew so intimately. It was in this mission to preserve Black male life that we bonded and established mutual respect; a relationship that nurtured our collaboration on this work twenty years later.

With the benefit of hindsight, each contributor to this pivotal work understands the value of controlling their narrative. In each essay, you will discover a common theme that permeates every stage and each choice that plays out in the journey to a fully realized humanity – the quest to be seen, *heard, and affirmed.* Whether it be childhood neglect, pursuing wealth at any cost, or the depths we are willing to go to garner mere respect, they all rotate on the axis of these three needs. From childhood to adulthood, we witness each man closing the gap between the myths that have come to suffocate their existence and the stories that authentically reflect their humanity. Between these pages, the frustration of proving we are more than what is perceived comes into perspective. Life's humility tempers the consuming hatred that dictates the pain we inflict on those we love. Each man discovers the limitations of the will and reconciles with the process of the journey.

As an actor, part of my training is being aware that each person I encounter embodies numerous stories that influence their behavior. The person I see before me represents a convergence of culture, trauma, socialization, and countless other factors. All the unseen life that animates and motivates each person is identified as the subtext. For multiple reasons, we allow some factors to wield more power than others, and our behavior reflects those choices. This work is an invitation to encounter the subtext we are denied when passing a Black man on the street. We learn the circumstances that inform the life and choices that make each man unique. With these stories we can begin creating new myths, based on truth, to effectively dismantle the harmful narratives that undermine the fulsome humanity of Black men.

Sekou Laidlow is a professional actor, ordained clergy, and podcast host. He is on the Board of Directors for Beautiful Ventures, a creative social enterprise that influences popular culture, disrupts anti-blackness, and elevates perceptions of Black humanity. To learn more about his work, visit https://www.sekoulaidlow.com/.

GOD'S GOT A CALLING ON MY LIFE

by Carlton Hurdle

THE YOUNGEST OF EIGHT

Growing up as the baby in my family was tough. I was the youngest of eight children and had one brother and six sisters, which wasn't easy to deal with. My mother only has one sister, an identical twin, and my father had five brothers and one sister, all from the same generation as my dad. Growing up, I was blessed to have my grandparents on both sides. I remember when we used to go to my dad's parent's house almost every weekend, and on the way, we always passed my mom's sister's house. My dad always told my mom before we loaded up the car to head out, "I'm going to stop to see your folks before I go to my mom's house." And even though my dad told my mom this, we unfortunately never did.

However, off we'd go with Dad driving about 20 miles over the speed limit and my mom always saying, "You know, we got these kids in this car, you need to slow down." As we were passing cars, my pops focused on the road ahead, his mind set on the destination. He always told her that we weren't going to stay at his parents' house long...with a big smile on his face that my mom referred to as his "side smile."

As I was the baby of the bunch, I had to sit in the middle of my six sisters. That was like walking in a minefield because I always fell asleep and got tortured by them. They called me "truck head" because my head was bigger than my body and they pushed it from one side to the other, lip gloss was put on my lips...you name it, it happened. When the car finally reached my grandparents' house, I got out of that car and ran like a lion was chasing me! Free at last, free at last!

One thing that I loved about my grandmother was that she always had food prepared when we arrived. My grandparents had a farm with all kinds of animals – chickens, pigs, geese, and cornfields as far as the eye could see. We had a great time but when nighttime fell, it was not so great for me. They had an outhouse so we had to go outside in the dark to use the bathroom. For me, being the youngest, about 11 years old at the time, it was like being in a horror movie...no lights in sight, and of course they always had to talk about somebody that had recently died. By that point, I'd be done while sitting next to my dad, about to pull his leg off.

As it got late, we would load up the car to head back home. However, we weren't going to get out of there easily. My grandma always said something to scare us and make our hair stand up on our bodies. She would stand up and kiss all of us before we exited through the back door that faced the outhouse. She would tell my dad, "Drive safe, but when you get to that road over the canal bank and see that lady with the cow, keep going through her and don't stop." After that, the race was on between me and my sisters to see who could get on the floor in the back of the car, first. Being at the bottom was the best spot because everyone else blocked the view. My dad would drive down Highway 17 so fast that if there was a lady with a cow crossing the road – and we named her "the glass eye lady with a cow" – she got out of my pop's way, for sure!

These were fun times with my family as we were so close back then. Mom and Dad always kept us safe and kept a roof over our heads. Many of my friends only had one parent but I was fortunate to grow up with both of my parents. Dad was always there and always provided for us.

GROWING UP IN THE PROJECTS

Growing up in the projects, as a little kid with six sisters and one brother, I felt safe when they were around until I had to go off on my own to school or to the park to play. As you can imagine, there was always that group of kids or boys that made fun of you, called you a mama's boy, or asked, "Where is your brother or sisters now?" In particular, there were two brothers that I was afraid of who always bullied the kids in the park. The youngest one would pick a fight with you but would then run to his older brother, who could really fight. I'd seen him break the arm of a boy he was fighting on the basketball court. I knew I could fight but when I saw that, my shoulders shook up and down and I said to myself, "I ain't never gonna fight that boy."

However, one day we were playing marbles and the youngest one took my marbles. I forgot about his older brother and pushed him down. As I walked home, I quickly became afraid that his brother was going to break my arm too. Later that day, while sitting on my back porch, I heard some boys say, "It's going to be a fight after school tomorrow on bus #54." I realized that was the bus I rode home every day, so I wondered if they were talking about me. I told myself, "Oh boy! I can't let everybody see me get beat up tomorrow."

So, later that night, I started looking at a karate book that my brother had given me and I began to practice some moves. I felt ready to defend myself as I hit my mattress and kicked the arms on my mom's couch. However, the next day on the bus ride home from school, I forgot all about my training. There were kids that didn't even stay in my neighborhood who rode bus #54 that day. Well, you can imagine what happened next... When the doors to the bus opened, I was the first one off, and I ran as fast as I could with both of them chasing me. I made it home and ran into the house, not knowing my dad was home. He was usually never home at that time of day. My dad looked at me and said, "Boy, what are you running from, slamming my door like you're crazy?" At that point, a voice coming from outside said, "Come outside, we're going to beat you up." My dad told me I had a choice to make. "Either you can go outside and face those brothers or face me. My son don't run from nobody." My legs were shaking and I was sweating and scared to death when my dad opened the door and told those brothers, "Y'all want to fight my son? That's fine, but only one of you gonna fight him at a time." I looked for the youngest brother to step forward, but that didn't happen. The "arm breaker" stepped forward... As I looked back at my dad, he just nodded his head. I went outside swinging like a young boy with a sugar rush and came out victorious.

Back in the day, when you got into a fight, the next day it was like nothing happened. But something did happen to me. The "arm breaker" eventually became my best friend. Sometimes I wished that I had never fought him because he was "the park's little thug" and his uncles and cousins were big-time drug dealers. At an early age, I had seen things and was introduced to things that a 12-year-old, little 98-pound boy should have never seen. I became popular by hanging around the older thugs who had all kinds of guns and drugs, although I never did any drugs at this age. I was also around a lot of drinking and numbers-running houses, and I would take numbers on a piece of paper to houses thinking it was a phone number. I also went to crap houses where dice were being played and held money for some of the big-time winners so they wouldn't lose all their money at one time. And I heard language that would burn your ears off.

I was so innocent when I was around my parents and sisters, but on the weekends, my brother held card games and dice shooting games, so I always hung out with him because he kept money in my pockets. He didn't realize that his baby brother was becoming a little gangster. I was quite different from my siblings because no one could make me do anything that I didn't want to do. I always told my mom that I was going to be different than those boys in the hood, but hanging around the "arm breaker", I thought hood life was normal. As I made a name for myself, all the teenage boys would call me "Big C" because I was "the man" back then, at a young age.

Summertime rolled around and my pops told me, "School is out now, and you need to find a summer job." I said okay because no matter what, I respected my parents. So, I got a job at McDonald's, about a mile from our house, and walked to work every day. I worked hard at McDonald's until the "arm breaker" and his uncle came there one day. They looked at me and said, "You don't have to work here, you can have this," and showed off hundreds of dollars.

I knew right from wrong because I came from a religious family. My parents were always in church. I remember when I was first introduced to weed, I never had to buy it because I hung around older dudes who sold it, so I always had weed in my pocket and got all my friends high. I didn't smoke it that much because the smell would stay on me and my eyes would be bloodshot red. When I went around my mom, she always said, "You better not be smoking those stems." I asked my mom, "What are stems?" She looked at me and replied, "Don't be funny." She would slap me so fast that Clint Eastwood didn't have anything on her, but I always respected her.

I lived in a house with praying parents and a father who sang in a professional quartet. I attended church every Sunday, followed by going to quartet singing programs, but on Monday through Saturday, I was being overtaken by influence, living a secret life my parents didn't know about.

I played all recreational sports and was good at all of them but got caught up with the hood life in the projects that I thought was normal. Seeing our neighbors the first of each month looking out the window, standing on the porch, waiting to see if the mail truck was coming to deliver a check and food stamp vouchers, was the life I knew well.

A THUG'S LIFE

There I was, trying to be hard six days a week while my parents were always praying that we wouldn't get caught up with the wrong people. It had gotten to the point that every time I would leave the house, my mom would ask me, "Boy, where you going?" And off I'd go to the basketball court. We played from sunup until sundown. Just as my team was beginning to win back-to-back games, my mom would come to the door and yell at me, "Boy, come take out the trash." Running home at top speed, while my team took a break as I dumped the trash, I at one time thought my name was Trash Man. We had a total of ten people in our household which I guess is why we had so much trash. After going to empty the trash that day, on my way back to the basketball court, I experienced three things in my life that made me grow up fast.

A couple of buildings down, I saw one of my homeboys sitting on his porch and he had just overdosed. I had never seen anything like that, in person. His eyes had rolled back in his head, he was shaking like a leaf on a tree, and there was a bubble in the vein in his arm, the size of a golf ball. For some odd reason, the "church boy" came out of me. I walked to the other side of the fence and began to pray, hiding from my friends so they wouldn't call me "church boy" because I was "Big C" and I couldn't let anybody think that I was soft.

The second thing I experienced occurred one day while I was crossing the street in front of a house that we had named "the corner house." The park bully came out and yelled, "Why are you so close to my house?" and punched me twice in the chest. When I looked around, everybody was watching, including my homeboys from the basketball court. Then out of nowhere, the "arm breaker" stepped out of the crowd and handed me a baseball bat, and before I knew it, I hit that boy in the neck not knowing how hard I had hit him, and then I ran home. The next thing I heard was an ambulance siren and I thought it was the police coming to get me, as I looked out my bedroom window, scared to death. My mom yelled upstairs, "What happened?" As a terrified kid, I replied, "I don't know."

Later that night, the park bully's family showed up at our door. They also had a large family with about the same number of sisters that I had. His mom was in a rage, screaming, "Your son hit my boy in the throat with a baseball bat and damaged his vocal cords, and he's in the hospital!" Then one of his sisters said, "We going to beat somebody up tonight for what your cowardly brother did." As my parents were Christians, they apologized, but that did not sit well with my sisters.

That night, while my parents were sleeping in their room downstairs, my older sister, the fighter, talked my other sisters into following her. My dad had put locks on our doors at the house that were so secure that Houdini couldn't even get out. So, my sisters climbed out of the upstairs window to fight that boy's sisters who had come to my house. One thing I can say about my sisters is that they really could fight because when you fought one, you would have to fight them all. They were very well known in the projects as "The Hurdle Girls." My sisters were in many fights and always came out undefeated.

The next day as I proceeded to the basketball court, I heard a lot of noise and suddenly, I saw the boy that had got in a fight with the "arm breaker." He, and three carloads of boys, jumped out and began to shoot at the basketball court, not aiming at anyone, but everybody who was in the way. We ran so fast! I could hear the bullets hitting the pavement and telegram poles, and cars that weren't even in the way got hit. As I ran to find a place to hide, I said, "Lord, don't let me go out this way." I was about 15 years old at that time. The next day, I was so scared because the "arm breaker" was my friend, and I knew they were coming for me next. However, I ended up crossing the path of one of the boys that were in the cars shooting at us and he told me, "Big C, you are cool, leave that chump (referring to the "arm breaker") alone. From now on, your name is Cottonball."

SMOOTHIE AND THE CHURCH BOY

Suddenly, I was living a thug's life. I was undercover, still going to church with my parents every Sunday, hiding weed in my room, taking advice from some of the older thugs in my hood, playing the innocent role around my family as "baby boy" or "little brother", but there was something different about me. I had seen guys get beat up badly, girls who got beat up by their boyfriends and even saw my sister get mistreated by boys. I wanted to hurt them so badly, but I couldn't reveal who I really was at the age of 16. I used to walk around with a sawed-off shotgun strapped to my leg but no one knew this, and they used to call my dad, "Shotgun Shorty." I guess the apple doesn't fall far from the tree.

When the summer ended, I went off to school, as a sophomore, and by this time, I had a new name, "Smoothie" – skinny, dark-skinned, and not afraid of anyone. My baby sister was in school with me during that time and she would tell my mom everything

I did until she became the captain of the flag squad, which took up so much of her time that she couldn't tell on me.

I began to play basketball and football until one day, a senior told me, "You're too good-looking to play football, you don't look like the type." However, with my hood mentality, I still got hooked up with the wrong boys in school. Some days school was good and some days it was bad because we used to get high in the mornings before classes, and on the weekends, it was really on. Through all of this, I still maintained my schoolwork because my parents didn't play that.

When the weekends came around, my homeboys and I had plenty of weed, and we got high in the parks or wherever we could hide the car so no one would see us. One day, there were about five of us in the car getting high, laughing, telling jokes to each other, talking about which girls we'd had or were trying to get, and suddenly, I looked at everybody in the car and said, "Let's pray." I didn't know the church boy was going to come out of me at that time. Well, you know, it got so quiet in that car...everybody was high, looking at each other, and then the laughter began again. They looked at me and said, "Church boy, you need to get out, you're blowing our high." They all knew I had a sawed-off shotgun strapped to my leg, so I took the shotgun out, and suddenly, it got quiet again...and I prayed.

We laughed, but something happened in that car that night. The next day, we all just looked at each other and said, "You good?" We had developed such a bond, that when you saw one of us, you'd see all five of us. We went to house parties and school dances together, and we were a five-man gang, but only one of us had a car, and we called him 6'9 because he was very tall. We all stayed in the same housing project. When we described ourselves as "going with a girl", we all knew because we only dated the girls in our hood, until we went to high school and met girls from everywhere. The race was on and I had a lot of girlfriends that weren't from my hood.

Playing sports and living a thug life wasn't easy, as I walked around high school wearing baggy pants, trying to hide a sawed-off shotgun strapped to my leg, thinking I was hard. Until, one Sunday night, my parents went to an outside revival and the preacher walked over to me and said, "You don't have to walk around like that; God's got a calling on your life." Well, something happened to me that night.

The next morning was Monday and time to go to school, but for some odd reason, the gun wouldn't stay strapped to my leg so I left it at home and hid it very well because my mom always cleaned my room. In school that day, I felt exceptionally light. Looking at everyone, I thought someone was going to start a fight with me, but as time went on, I began to not miss that gun. I ended up giving it back to my homeboys in the hood. Then they told me I was getting soft. "I'm Big C, so why don't you try me if you think I'm getting soft," is what I would say. Later that night, some of my homeboys got into a fight, so, off I went, knowing that life was not for me anymore. I said to myself, "This will be the last fight for me."

I am so glad that I had praying parents because two of my friends died that night. All that night, I was thinking about what that preacher said at the revival, that God had a calling on my life. Two Sundays after that, I went to hear my dad sing with his quartet called The Hurdle Brothers. Before the program got started, the pastor was praying and he looked at me and said, "Young man, you've got a calling on your life." I know my mom said that she prayed for me while she was pregnant with me, that I would be a great man of God. But for some reason, all these pastors began to scare me because, in all the churches I visited, they said the same thing, "You've got a calling on your life." I was thinking, "I'm too young for this, I want to get high and drunk, and party with my girlfriend and my homeboys. So, I stopped going to church for years because I didn't want to hear that anymore. I was a thug, Big C, Smoothie!

THE REMINISCENCE

We had a great time back then, growing up in the hood because we were like one big, happy family. We fought but the next day we were friends again. During the summer holidays, cookouts were awesome, especially around the first of the month because there were a lot of people in the project on welfare who received food stamps. I was blessed to have a dad that worked every day and who provided for all eight of us...until he couldn't.

I remember that on one summer day, my dad and I were on the front porch repairing a fan when my dad grabbed his chest. He had a heart attack. I picked my dad up and put him in the car even though I'd never driven a car before, except to pull it around back to wash it. However, on that day, I drove my dad to the emergency room, about five miles away. After this happened, my dad was not able to work for a while, so on some Friday nights, my parents hosted house parties to raise money to help buy school clothes for the eight of us. I was too young to attend but I would look around the corner from the top of the stairs, and I thought everyone was nasty because I didn't understand slow dragging (as they called it back then). However, as I got older, I thought slow dragging was the bomb!

I remember around Christmas time when I was very young, the Salvation Army used to come to our hood with boxes of food, and they were going to give us only one box until they looked inside our house and said, "With all these kids, you all need two boxes."

That year on Christmas Eve, I walked upstairs to my room, scared to death because my parents said, "If you do not go to bed and go to sleep, Santa's going to put pepper in your eyes." When I woke up the next morning, I heard kids playing outside. Excited, I ran downstairs to see what Santa had brought me but didn't see anything, and I wondered, "Why did Santa skip our house?" Since Santa was my dad and he hadn't worked for a while because of his heart attack, Christmas didn't come to our house the way it used to. However, thanks to the Salvation Army, my mom was able to cook a great Christmas dinner.
Experiencing hardships after my dad could no longer work, made me realize that I wanted to be different and make my parents proud of me. There were many nights we didn't have food and it was difficult for me, as a young boy, to understand why. My mom never complained but made the best meals with whatever was in the cabinets, seemingly out of nothing.

THE MIRACLE THAT TRANSFORMED ME

I can honestly say that even with all the challenges I've faced in my life, God has always been there. I met my wife, Sonja, during my junior year in high school. We got married at 19 years old and throughout 36 years of marriage, we have been hit with a lot of stuff that could have destroyed our marriage. I was unfaithful, jealous, hung out with drug dealers, and my wife could have walked away, but God didn't let her. I thought I had missed out on something by getting married so young.

One day while walking to the mailbox, I met an elderly lady who said, "Hold your head up young man, God's got a calling on your life and that's why you are getting hit hard. The enemy wants you to think that the other side of the road is good, but God is going to keep whipping you because he loves you. My son-in-law has a church around the corner, and you should go visit."

The next Sunday, I went to visit this church and during prayer, the pastor started walking the aisles and I was thinking to myself, "Lord please don't let him stop here by me." Sure enough, he did, and looked over at me and said, "God's got a calling on your life." I did not go back to that church for a long time.

The next Friday night, my wife and I were playing cards when I started to feel dizzy and it was difficult for me to breathe, so I told my wife to get me to the hospital, quickly. We arrived at the emergency room and when they looked at me, they took me straight to the back and began to do x-rays and CT scans on me, and in about an hour I was told, "You need to get in touch with your family because your condition could be fatal. You have blood clots in your lungs the size of golf balls, and you should try to stay as still as possible." I was terrified when I heard this and I began to call on the name of Jesus! I told the Lord, "I surrender...no more. God, I know that I have a calling on my life," and he began to show me all the people I had hurt, all the families I had destroyed, the kids that went hungry when I sold their parents drugs and took food from their mouths, and I cried out, "I surrender now."

Later that night, after they dimmed all the lights in my room so I could rest while they tried to figure out what to do next, a dark figure stood over me and I felt myself drifting away, just like a fighter does when he gets knocked out. But I wasn't ready to give up, and suddenly, a bright figure lied on top of me and I heard the Lord say, "I heard your cry and it's sincere." Right away, I felt better.

The next day, I told the doctors and nurses I was okay and asked them to retest me. As I was lying in the hospital bed, looking out the window, repenting for all the things I'd done in my life, a white dove suddenly appeared in my window and a sense of peace was restored over me. God had sent an angel my way to let me know that everything was alright.

As I began to get comfortable, I heard a noise in the hallway. It was my family who had arrived at the hospital. I have never seen my family come to Atlanta so fast! It's so amazing how God works and how he shows us his work. When my family entered my room, three doctors followed behind them and they had my test results. The doctors hung them on the board in the room and showed my test results from the night before, holding the CT scan, the MRI, and x-rays, in front of the light. They looked at each other amazed. "This is what we saw two days ago Mr. Hurdle, and this is what we're seeing after we re-tested you. We don't understand, but we cannot find any blood clots in your lungs on these new results."

I went from the emergency room to the ICU, to home the next day. When God's calling on your life and shows you all the mistakes you've made and all the people you've hurt, when the enemy thought he'd won, it's a remarkable thing. Even if your arm drops two times (I'm a wrestling fan) ...on the third one, God lifted my arm and it stayed up. That let me know that I am a champion. No person or thing can take your belt when God gives it to you.

Writing this story was a challenge for me because sometimes I've felt defeated and sometimes I've felt depressed, especially during this pandemic. I lost a cousin, my dad's youngest brother, and I'm still missing my dad whom I lost three years ago. My father always told me that, "I'm the positive and you are the negative." At first, I didn't understand this because no one wants to be the negative, but after he began to explain, it made a lot of sense. He told me that if a car battery goes dead, you can hook the positive up to the battery terminal by itself, but nothing will happen. However, when you connect the negative and positive together, you can jumpstart a freight train. That lets me know that when my battery gets low sometimes, I can connect my terminal to a higher calling, which is in Jesus Christ, and he lets me know that I am victorious! You are a champion when you connect with Jesus Christ because you win every time.

Stay with God!

ABOUT
CARLTON HURDLE

Carlton Hurdle was ordained on July 25, 2004, as a Minister of the Gospel. He has been married to his high school sweetheart, Sonja, for 36 years. He is the youngest of eight siblings and was born in Portsmouth, Virginia, where he grew up living in project housing. Despite the many hardships he faced as a young man growing up in the hood, he was determined to rise above his circumstances to live a life without limits. Over the years, he has developed a unique communication style that has given him the ability to take complex subjects and transpose them into easy to understand messages. As a Certified Mentor, his passion is to reach those individuals that have struggled throughout life to overcome obstacles and live the abundant life of God's promises.

Minister Carlton was chosen by his pastor to lead the men's ministry for several years at his church and planned events to encourage the men and bring them closer to Jesus Christ. His gift to connect with individuals of all ages and on all levels has brought him before great people, as he continues to captivate folks by sharing his testimony, being a witness of God's Glory, and preaching the gospel.

I AM NOT FINISHED YET!

by Willie L. Brown

MY LIFE, THE EARLY YEARS

I was born on August 15, 1962, in New Haven, Connecticut, the firstborn son of Willie L. Brown Sr. and Dorothy E. Brown. My parents moved from the south to the north looking for jobs and opportunities. My father found work in the factories, while my mother began working as a clerk typist. My dad worked hard and played hard. He was a good provider who brought his money home, but he liked to drink. Alcohol became his friend and our enemy. My mother was a fun-loving woman who kept people in stitches. I think I got my comedy gift from her. My father was serious, smart, and very methodical. He counted his pennies and made sure that we always had what we needed.

On March 11, 1966, my brother Eric was born, making me the big brother. We belonged to Emmanuel Baptist Church in New Haven, CT, but when we moved to Hamden my parents stopped attending regularly. My parents bought a house on 29 North Sheffield Street as they sought to give us a better environment to grow up in. Back then, a dollar would go a long way. I remember one time I took a dime from my mother's pocketbook and she gave me a hundred-dollar butt whipping. I never stole anything ever again.

LOVE AND DISCIPLINE

My mother was a strict disciplinarian, and she didn't play. Looking back, I thank her for it because she made us more afraid of her than we were of the people in the street. That discipline kept us out of jail. Growing up on North Sheffield St. sheltered us; our parents could find us in about ten minutes. We were either playing basketball down the street or playing softball on Millrock Road.

BUSED TO WHITE SCHOOLS

In the early 70s, we were the first to be bused to an all-white elementary school at Ridge Hill in Hamden. Fortunately, we didn't face much open racism until we got to middle school. It was strange how we all got along with each other in elementary school, but as soon as we got to Junior High it was "niggers suck" and "whiteboy." I remember a car full of older white guys driving fast down Morse St. yelling "Niggers" and throwing a bottle of beer at us. We would shrug it off like, "Yeah, y'all better keep going."

ALCOHOL, THE ENEMY WITHIN

My father was a great person when he wasn't drinking but once he got started, he changed. I could tell when he had been drinking too much because he would slur his words and breathe heavily. He used to come home late at night and start arguments with my mother, waking us up, cussing real loud. It was frightening. His drinking had become so bad that my mother moved us out of our house, and we went to live with my Aunt Cat in Westville for a while. My dad had a real problem, and everyone knew it. I wish that he would have gotten help or gone to Alcoholics Anonymous. The sad thing about it is that I didn't know that I would be plagued with a similar form of addiction myself later on in life.

BAPTIZED

When I turned 12, my father told me that I needed to give my life to Christ and get baptized. I think it was great that he suggested that I go to church, but it would have even been better if he would have taken me. My friends and I started going to Christian Tabernacle Baptist Church. I got baptized and joined the youth choir but didn't attend regularly because no one pushed me or made me go.

SPORTS, MAGIC, AND VENTRILOQUISM

We gained our freedom through organized sports. My mother came to all our basketball games, but my father never made it. I guess he was too busy working. At the time, I was introduced to the art of magic and fell in love with it. My interest in magic led me to ventriloquism. At the age of 13, I was inspired by Jay Johnson, a ventriloquist on the hit sitcom *Soap*. My mother bought me a Willie Talk dummy for Christmas and I learned the basics of how to throw my voice. Later, I found a home study course on ventriloquism in the back of a comic book and began to practice every day. I then ordered a semi-professional dummy.

One day the UPS man rang the doorbell and said, "I have a COD package for Willie Brown and that will be one hundred thirty-seven dollars." My father was like, "One hundred thirty-seven dollars for what?" I replied, "I'm getting a dummy, Dad." He said, "A dummy, a dummy, boy you the dummy, they took your money, they saw you coming!" I laughed to myself and was like, "Yeah, okay, whatever, you'll see."

My first show was at Nationwide Insurance Company where my mother worked as a Claims Adjuster. The show was a hit and people began to ask me how much I charged. One show led to another and I never stopped. At the age of 15, I talked my parents into letting me go to the National Ventriloquist Convention in Fort Mitchell, Kentucky by myself. I flew to Cincinnati and caught a shuttle over to the Drawbridge Motor Inn. I checked into the hotel with the convention guests and nobody asked me any questions about how old I was or where my parents were. I entered the Junior Competition and won first place, and received the Most Promising Ventriloquist Award.

PEER PRESSURE

Seeing that my basketball career ended so early I began to find interest in other things. A friend across the street introduced me to marijuana. I remember not wanting to smoke it at first, but I gave into peer pressure. We also began drinking quarts of Miller beer along with smoking. I didn't think it was a big deal because I was still doing well in school, and I was working at Yale New Haven Hospital in the kitchen. I would hang out with the older guys and it made me feel even more grown-up. I was doing everything that I was big and bad enough to do.

Getting high on weed and alcohol seemed to go right along with what the other kids were doing. It made me feel different and gave me the courage to talk to girls and dance at parties. I was a late bloomer and shy in that area, but I was destined to make up for it. Life was a blur during those last two years of high school. I would go to school and then go to work, hang out with a few of my friends, and go home. I'd usually be high and would head straight to my room so I wouldn't be confronted by my parents. One day, my father found some weed in the car and had my mother confront me. They took away my driving privileges until I could rebuild their trust. I continued to smoke but was a little more careful.

COLLEGE YEARS AT HAMPTON UNIVERSITY

Somehow, by the grace of God, I got accepted into college at Hampton University in Hampton, Virginia. Hampton University is one of the leading HBCUs in the nation and I majored in Mass Media Arts. I received a great education and a wonderful life experience. While at Hampton, I gained my independence and became a man. I was popular on campus from entering the talent shows and began booking shows with the fraternities and sororities. I was even booking shows and winning contests at nightclubs in Norfolk and Newport News. I did well academically during my first couple of years. I became a student leader in my sophomore year, and I also pledged Kappa Alpha Psi Fraternity Inc. Pledging made you feel like a celebrity on campus. It made us popular with the girls and the guys, 'cause the girls wanted us, and the guys wanted to be like us.

COLLEGE SWEETHEART, YOUNG LOVE

While at Hampton I met my college sweetheart, Wanda Shaw. She was an R.A. in Harkness Hall, one of the girls' dormitories. We dated for two years before she graduated and went back home to Capitol Heights, Maryland. One day, I received a call from Wanda, and she had some very surprising news to tell me. She was pregnant and the baby was due around October 1984, the year that I was to graduate.

YOUNG FAMILY WITH RESPONSIBILITY

After we found out that we had a baby girl on the way, we immediately told our families. To make things look halfway decent, we got married in April, a month before I would graduate. After graduation, I moved from Hampton, Virginia to Forestville, Maryland. Within a few days, we had our apartment. Wanda was working as an Apparel Manager for Kmart Corporation. I was unemployed but very hopeful. I quickly landed a couple of jobs in telemarketing in Arlington, Virginia, and before I knew it, I was working for Xerox Corporation in Bethesda, Maryland. God was working things out for my good. I could see that things were beginning to look up as long as I didn't get in the way.

XEROX AND MOONLIGHTING

On September 28, 1984, our beautiful daughter LaJuan was born. I was now in full swing at Xerox. I had some good years – made President's Club, won trips and awards – but I began to fall into a rut. I was starting to feel a lot of pressure and I was also moonlighting at nightclubs doing comedy. I got caught up in the trappings of show business. To my demise, I began to drink more heavily, smoke weed regularly, and began to do cocaine with some of the comedians after the shows. I became infatuated with the business and all it had to offer. I was working with comedians like Dave Chappelle, Wanda Sykes, and Chris Thomas, to name a few. Not everyone was doing drugs, but there was a select group of us who were. The late nights on stage and hanging out started to take a toll on me and my career at Xerox. My substance abuse had also begun to affect my marriage to Wanda.

I started going to Alcoholics Anonymous meetings at Andrews Air Force Base in Camp Springs, Maryland. That is where I first got sober. I stayed sober for a year or so before I started using again. I didn't know that alcohol and drug addiction was a progressive disease. I probably inherited it naturally from my father, and his father, and so forth. However, when you mix alcohol, weed, and cocaine, that is not a combination for success. Finally, I resigned from Xerox. I was fighting my demons and wanted to do better but I couldn't. I had even begun to experiment with crack cocaine and that was a horrible adventure, it was like the devil was trying to take me out. I remember going to church and paying my tithes, but I would still be smoking crack.

SHOW BIZ AND MARRIAGE

On October 12, 1989, my son Willie III was born. I'm happy to say that my son never saw me drunk, high, or under the influence. I was doing comedy full-time and had appeared nationally on *Comic View* on BET and *Russell Simmons' Def Comedy Jam* on HBO. The industry was starting to open up for black comedians and

I began to travel all over the country to perform. I was picking up shows everywhere and opening for artists like Frankie Beverly & Maze, Gladys Knight, Boyz II Men, and more. I also worked with comedians Mike Epps, Steve Harvey, Cedric the Entertainer, Martin Lawrence, Katt Williams, Bruce-Bruce, and the list goes on.

Over time, the travel, the ups and downs of the business, infidelity, and issues about money destroyed our marriage. We filed for bankruptcy and foreclosed on our house. I picked up and relocated to Los Angeles, California. Wanda and my children stayed behind. She was no longer feeling me or my dream. I guess not. Truth be told, I had put her through a lot of heartache and disappointment with my substance abuse.

THE HOLLYWOOD SHUFFLE

While on the road performing, I met a girl named Denise Wills from Clarksville, Tennessee. We hooked up and I ended up taking her on the road with me to Los Angeles. I was supposed to move in with my frat brother, Cornell Stephenson, but because I had Denise with me, I had to get my own place. The problem was that my credit was shot, and Denise didn't have any money or credit either. I met with the rental manager and he told me that I would have to pay the first month's rent and security deposit and pass the credit check. I became very depressed at that moment thinking that I had just driven three days across the country and I might have to stay in a homeless shelter or something. I called my mother in desperation and told her my dilemma. My mother told me to pray. Somehow, after praying I felt a release. It was as if my faith was increasing.

Mr. Figus had tried to contact several of my creditors but couldn't reach anyone. The only person that I knew that he could talk to was Woody. So, I went to my car, grabbed my suitcase, and went inside the office along with Denise. I opened it up, took Woody out, and put him on my knee. I made Woody look at Mr. Figus and say, "Sir, you have a chance to make a difference in somebody's life today." "Do you live in there?" asked Mr. Figus, referring to the suitcase. Woody replied, "Yeah, I live in there, he lives in there, she lives in there, and it's crowded as hell! We need somewhere to stay!" Mr. Figus started laughing and said, "I'll tell you what, since you are a friend of Cornell's, I'll prorate you for May's rent and waive your security deposit. If you give me five hundred dollars today, and three hundred dollars in a couple of days, I'll give you the key tonight." Look at God!

WORKING AND THE COMEDY STORE

Denise and I didn't work out as expected. She ended up moving in with another friend. I was on a mission and was trying to break into Hollywood to see how far I could go. So, I took a job at Bally Total Fitness so that I wouldn't have to travel around the country as much. I was making just enough money to get by and pay my child support. I missed my kids, and I was depressed by being separated from Wanda after all those years. Fortunately, I was able to break into the World Famous Comedy Store on Sunset Blvd. and became a paid regular. Mitzi Shore, Pauly Shore's mother, liked me and took me in. My name was painted outside on the wall of fame. A lot of famous comedians came through there, like Richard Pryor, Eddie Murphy, and Robin Williams. It was a big deal for me.

JOINING PRICE CHAPEL AME CHURCH

Although I was out in L.A. pursuing my comedy and acting career, I knew it was important that I belonged to a local church. So, I joined Price Chapel A.M.E. on Slauson Boulevard. I became very active at Price Chapel where I was a member of the choir and later, became a member of the Steward Board. I knew that I needed a church home and I loved being able to go to the altar each week and leave my burdens there. Through it all, I knew that God was with me and that I owed everything to him. He made it possible for me to work, pay my bills, pay my child support, and pursue my craft.

GOD'S BLESSINGS

I was just about to lose Daniel Hoff as an agent because he needed some new pictures from me, and I was dragging my feet. I had new pictures taken and a week later, I booked a national commercial for American Airlines. I made over thirty thousand dollars from that one spot. Anyway, I had money in my pocket if I needed to rent a car since mine had been repossessed.

DATING AND MOVING ON

After my separation from Wanda, I found myself in several relationships with different women. They were all nice, but for some reason or another, they didn't last. I always found myself wanting to be with the woman I was with in the previous relationship. It was like I was trying to fix what went wrong. No matter what, I loved them all. The strange thing is that I always attracted women whose fathers were alcoholics. I knew I had issues and I really needed to work on myself. I was unfaithful and had no problem chasing women. It was a part of the comedy culture, so I thought. I realize now that I had been very immature when it came to relationships with women. I was a road comic who was used to being promiscuous.

TO THINE OWN SELF BE TRUE

My last relationship in L.A. was with Vee. She was a very nice woman with a man who wasn't ready to settle down. I think it had a lot to do with timing, and that I was still hurt over the breakup of my marriage to Wanda. Together, we produced a short film called *Footcops*. It was a comedy about two detectives who didn't have a car and had to fight crime on foot. Thanks to her, the film was entered into the Pan African Film Festival and was nominated for Best Short Film. Many popular comedians were a part of our film, including Rodney Perry, Reginald Ballard who played "Bruh-Man" on Martin, Buddy Lewis, Edwonda White, Retha Jones, T.J. McGee, Bobby Law, Annie McKnight, Vince D, and Derrick Ellis. Vee and I accomplished some great things together, but this relationship would take an emotional toll on both of us.

CLEAN COMEDY VS. BLUE COMEDY

By this time, I was back to full-time comedy and I had to decide between being clean all the time or being blue. I had been picked up by an agency called Outreach Comedy that would place me in churches all over the country each week. One of their rules was that you had to be clean all the time even if you weren't working for them. I was like, "Yeah, okay, whatever, I'm going to be me." One day I got a call from Dionne who was the head of the comedy department at Outreach asking me if I had appeared on television using blue comedy. I lied to her and told her that it wasn't me. I remember feeling so bad about that. My conscience bothered me. I had let God down, his people, and myself. I felt like I was no better than Peter in the Bible and that I had denied Christ. A couple of days later I called Dionne and told her that I misrepresented the agency and that it was me on television using blue humor. She said, "Willie, I'm so glad that you came back and told me the truth. You are really the type of person that we want on our roster. If you promise to adhere to our clean comedy policy, we will continue to work with you." That was the beginning of a new walk for me. I could no longer just talk the talk, I needed to walk the walk.

HERE COMES THE SON

Life was moving along steadily out in Cali. I was going on auditions, going to my A.A. meetings, going to church, and seeing Vee off and on. One day I got a call from Wanda saying that our son Willie III was getting out of hand and that he needed to come to live with me. I knew that he needed to be with me, I just didn't know how I was going to pull it off. Just before he moved out to L.A., all my comedy work dried up. I guess God was making a way for my son. I had to take a job driving limo to make ends meet, but it gave me the flexibility to drop my son off at school and take him to church to be with the young peoples' department. The time I spent in the limo gave me a chance to read the Bible, pray, and spend more time with God. My church family, along with a few trusted friends, helped me to take care of my son when I had to leave town. After about two months, things kicked back into gear and I was full-time again.

MOVING BACK EAST

In 2005, I decided to move back east. My son was becoming homesick and we needed a bigger place. I spoke to my friend, Gordon Robert's wife, Sandra, who was a realtor in Atlanta. She ran my credit and told me that I was qualified to purchase anything I wanted. Thirty days later, my son and I were driving across the country from L.A. to Atlanta. We went from a one-bedroom apartment to a four-bedroom house with a two-car garage on half an acre of land. "Won't He do it!"

Just before leaving L.A., I booked a recurring role on Showtime Network's *Barbershop*. It was a spin-off of Ice Cube's movie *Barbershop* and starred Omar Gooding as Calvin, the barbershop owner. My agent Leigh Castle sent me to an audition with casting director Robi Reed, a fellow Hamptonian. They were looking for a guy to play a homeless veteran ventriloquist with an overly religious dummy. I booked it! The very next day I was on the Paramount lot, shooting.

A NEW LIFE

God is amazing. Through all I had been through: addiction, foreclosure, bankruptcy, car repossession, divorce, separation from my children, living alone on the other side of the country, God still allowed me to elevate. As Biggie said, "I went from ashy to classy." In January 2006, my mother moved in with me and my son. She became the nucleus of the house and kept us both grounded to a certain degree. Unfortunately, my son got in trouble with weed and was going down the same path that I had been on, but even worse. His inability to stop using landed him in jail and eventually out of my house. I truly loved my son, and I gave him everything I had. I believed in my heart that one day he would find that to be true.

MY SHERRY AMOUR

I met my wife Sherry on a Christian cruise sponsored by Harlequin Christian author Kendra Norman Bellamy. I worked as the comedian, and Sherry performed as the mime dancer. When the ship docked, a small group of us would go on excursions. I got to know Sherry and when we returned to land, I booked her on a few engagements with me. She worked for Delta and could fly for free. She began accompanying me to my shows out of town and we became a serious item. We dated for about a year or so before I moved her and her daughter Kyerica into the house with me and my mother. I proposed to her and we got married. I felt complete and Sherry made me feel confident that I could marry again. I believe that I helped her feel the same way as well.

I realized that I had wanted to be married for a long time, but I just wasn't the right person. Sherry's love for God and myself affirmed me and helped me to see myself in a better light. Through our relationship and spiritual growth, I saw that I could be faithful to her, and knew that I could be the man that God wanted me to be.

CHRISTIAN MISSION

Having Sherry by my side gave me more motivation to grow spiritually and accomplish more than ever. We ran Youth Vision Builders Inc., a mentor program for children living in the McDonough Housing Authority. We also produced Gospel Comedy Live, which was a standup comedy show for Christian comedians. Also during this time, Sherry acted as my road manager as I was traveling and opening up for gospel recording artists like David and Tamela Mann from Tyler Perry's *Meet the Browns*, Marvin Sapp, Yolanda Adams, Deitrick Haddon, and many others. I appeared on the Radio One, One Love Cruise, and toured with Shelly Garrett's play *Beauty Shop*. Consequently, I was running The Clean Comedy Clinic Inc., a booking agency for clean and Christian comedians.

SO LONG DAD, BYE MOM

When you lose both parents you often wonder what this life will be without them. I can only be thankful that I had them, and that they gave me everything they had to give. In April 2013, I received a call from my Aunt Janett telling me that I needed to come home to check on my dad. He had been suffering from fluid around his heart which caused him to have severe swelling in his feet and ankles. In a week I was able to get him the medical attention that he needed with nurses and home care aides. Before I left, he was admitted to the hospital and then released to a rehabilitation center. Within a few days, I was notified that he had passed.

At the end of life, I think what matters most to a parent is whether the people that you sacrificed much for would be there in your time of need. I'm proud to say that I was there for him. I remember one night where my brother Eric and I were getting ready to bathe our dad and he had a look of desperation in his eyes. He told me that he was sorry that we had to assist him, and I told him that it was okay and that it was the least that we could do for all that he had done for us. He laid back on the bed and we bathed him. He was satisfied. My father wasn't perfect, but he was still a great man in my eyes. He instilled so many wonderful qualities in me and my brother. Over time, he had become one of my biggest fans. He would often brag about me to his coworkers and they would tell him whenever they saw me on television. Bill Brown was a giant of a man and he would never be forgotten.

In 2016, we would revisit mortality with my dear mother Dorothy. My mom had become my best friend, supporter, confidante, and business partner. She was always there for me, and I had an opportunity to return the favor. She was able to spend the last ten years of her life living with me, and that was truly a gift. My wife Sherry assisted me in helping with my mom after she had her TIA. She would deal with the loss of memory and restricted mobility, and at times we had to bathe, clothe, and feed her. At the same time, I was pursuing a Master of Theology degree at Ohio Christian University, running our comedy business, and working as a network marketing affiliate in Karatbars International.

On March 28, 2016, I graduated from Ohio Christian University with my mother, daughter LaJuan, son Willie III, friend Curtis Butler III, and frat brother Howard K. Smith in attendance. Once again, my mother showed up at one of the biggest moments in my life. My wife Sherry was in Los Angeles at a Karatbars Conference but immediately following graduation, I rushed to the airport to fly out and meet her. On July 16, Sherry and I were returning from one of my engagements out of town. We planned to go and see my mother who at this time had moved to Elmcroft Nursing Home in Jonesboro. We were very tired on that day and decided that we would go see her the next day after church. At 5:00 a.m. I received a call from Elmcroft that my mother had been rushed to Southern Regional Hospital in Riverdale. We hurried over to the hospital and upon entering were notified that she had passed.

We identified her body and returned home to prepare for a show at Wesley Chapel AME Church in McDonough. By 11:00 a.m. I was on stage preaching and doing comedy. I'm sure my mother wouldn't have it any other way. Later, we made the arrangements to have my mother flown back home to New Haven, Connecticut. Through it all I have no regrets. God made it possible for me to be there for my parents when they needed me most. I am grateful for that gift. Many months went by before I even shed a tear for either of my parents. At times, I thought that something was wrong with me, or that maybe I was just trying to be tough for the family. I guess God had prepared me and was standing up inside of me. Everything that my parents were, is what I am, and I feel their presence in me every day. When I smile and laugh, I see my mother, and when I'm serious about something, I see my father.

WALKING IN MY PURPOSE

When you are walking in your purpose God will open doors for you and direct your path. For years, I thought that I was just cleaning up my comedy act for the church, but, God was cleaning me up for ministry. I would attend the annual Christian Comedy Conferences or CCA and remember meeting comedians who were pastors and ministers. I was intrigued by the thought of it and it jumped on me. One day I was reading Jeremiah 1 in which the Lord told Jeremiah that he would put his words in his mouth and tell him what to say. Something happened to me on that day. I realized that I was no longer just a comedian, but that I was a mouthpiece for God.

I think a lot of people run from their calling because they think they are not good enough. I believe that none of us are good enough on our own, but it is Christ who makes us good enough. God uses misfits, those who are scarred, those who have been lost, those who have been through something. While I knew that I had comedic talent and ability, it was time for me to not just tell jokes, but to preach and minister God's word. My wife and I have received numerous prophecies from people that we didn't know telling us that we were going to be a part of a huge move for Christ. They would say that we would be very influential in helping to save souls and ushering people into the Kingdom of God.

After my mother passed, I busied myself with work and ministry. At the beginning of the new year, I would put all my education and training to use by getting into my pastor's Ministry in Training Program at Tabernacle of Praise Church International in McDonough, Georgia. Pastor T.J. McBride led the ministers in training by teaching us and guiding us through scriptures, and books such as John Maxwell's 21 *Irrefutable Laws of Leadership, The Five Star Church, Whose Holding My Ladder*, and more. We went through a ten-month program which ultimately led to our ordination. The way I see it, nothing happens by accident. God knows exactly what he is doing. I love preaching God's word and I have a lot of respect for the craft. Every time I get up to do it, I get better. Therefore, I know that it's not just me, but it's the Holy Spirit that is making me better. What's great about this journey of life is that it is still unfolding. The word says that we go from faith to faith. In other words, more will be revealed.

STILL A CHAMPION

Although my life has been filled with many challenges and ups and downs, I feel that the good has far outweighed the bad. I was blessed to have two parents who cared about me and nurtured me. I was able to grow up safely as a child and to pursue education and my talents and gifts. I am the proud father of two biological children, three children by marriage, seven grandchildren, and one great-grandchild. I have a beautiful God-fearing wife and wonderful in-laws. I have developed an amazing relationship with my Uncle James, who is my father's oldest brother, and my Aunt Janett, my father's sister, and my Uncle Ronny. They are all a part of the tribe that raised me. It takes a village to raise a child and they did a great job, along with those who have gone on to glory.

I am an overcomer. I made it through substance abuse, alcoholism, sexual promiscuity, and still I rise. I defeated divorce, bankruptcy, foreclosure, repossession, and death. I overcame corporate America and became a full-fledged entrepreneur. I have traveled the world, done global missions in Haiti and South Africa, appeared nationally on television and film, and have met and worked with some of the biggest celebrities in the secular and gospel industry. And at the writing of this book, in the year 2020, I have endured one of the worst plagues known to man. Hundreds of thousands of people have died due to what is known as Covid-19 or Coronavirus. This pandemic has ravaged the entire world, changing life as we know it. It has single-handedly shut down our world economy, forcing people to stay home from work to shelter within. People of all ages are urged to wear masks, wash their hands constantly, use hand sanitizer, and observe social distancing rules and regulations. Churches, sporting events, entertainment venues, restaurants, and large gatherings have been closed.

Not only is the world going through this pandemic that is reminiscent of the Bird Flu of 1918; moreover, we are seeing the rise of racial injustice and police brutality at a level that is incomprehensible. With the murders of George Floyd, Breonna Taylor, Rayshard Brooks, Jacob Blake, and many others at the hands of the police, and the divisive nature of President Donald Trump, America is on a downward spiral of prejudice, bigotry, and moral decay. Thank God for Black Lives Matters, and the young people, Black, white, Asian, and Latino who have put their lives on the line to protest for a better way of life. But through it all, we are still finding a way to survive. Somehow, a lot of good will come out of this. God is using these situations to make us better. It has forced us to find out who we are, whose we are, and what we can do with what we have right now. Through it all, I survived, and I realize that I am not finished yet! I have a lot of work left to do. My mission is to use my gift of comedy and create positive images through media and film to encourage the family, and to introduce a dying world to a risen savior, Jesus Christ. In the words of the ring announcer, "In this corner with the black trunks, bald head, and sprinkled gray mustache and goatee, weighing in at two hundred fifty pounds, from New Haven, Connecticut, and still a champion... Willie L. Brown Jr.!!"

ABOUT
WILLIE L. BROWN

Willie L. Brown is a man with a mission. He just happens to be a sought after, nationally known comedian, ventriloquist, and minister of the gospel. You may have seen him on the best of BET's *Comic View, Def Comedy Jam* on HBO, Bounce TV's sitcom *Last Call, The Rickey Smiley Show*, or in the movie *All About You*. Brown didn't always start on the top. Like most, his life was met with many challenges. He's gone from addiction, divorce, and bankruptcy to recovery, fortune, and fame.

Brown uses his gift of comedy and ministry as a platform to win souls for Christ. His focus is to entertain and encourage families and individuals through social media, television, and film. He shows you that no matter what others say, you can succeed if you believe and never give up. Brown talks to men about standing up and being the King that God created them to be. He believes that men are the protectors and priests of their households and that it is their job to raise the next generation to be the same.

Be all you can be and realize that just because life beats you down doesn't mean that you can't win. Find your passion and strength against all odds and be the champion that you were destined to be. Willie L. Brown holds a Bachelor of Arts degree from Hampton University in Mass Media Arts and a Master of Theology from Ohio Christian University.

FROM THE PROJECTS TO THE PENTAGON

by Harold Holden

THE EARLY YEARS

I was born on May 3, 1966, in Fort Valley, Georgia. Fort Valley is the home of the Georgia Peach crop with a population of 8,500 people. When I was a kid, life was simple. I was raised by a single mother with four siblings, including my famous twin brother, and we were abandoned by our father. My dad, Ernest Holden, taught me a lot about what to do as a dedicated father and what not to do as an out of sight, out of mind father. My father abruptly left our family of five kids in 1967 with no notice or even a goodbye to his own family. We owe a debt of gratitude to my grandmother (on my father's side), Marjorie Edwards Thorpe, for assisting her very young daughter-in-law with raising and supporting five kids. My grandmother was an elementary school teacher for 36 years in Peach County. I think that my hard work ethic and behavior are directly inherited from her. She was a woman with perseverance and an awesome work ethic. "Mommie", as we affectionately called her, passed in 2004. May she rest in peace.

My dad proved to be irresponsible and quite immature when he decided to leave us as a young adult, for no known reason. The first time I saw my father in person, I was 13 years old. The moment I met him is not a great memory as he told my twin brother to be quiet as he gulped a pint of his favorite cheap liquor, vodka. That was not the way that I pictured meeting my dad. However, may God Bless his soul. He passed from multiple forms of cancer in July of 2009. As I said, there is something for everyone to learn in this world; both good and bad lessons. In the case of my father, the lessons were tough and filled with many heartbreaking moments and thoughts that add up to many disappointments. During my father's last days on Earth, I had a chance to spend some valuable moments with him as we prepared for his earthly transition. His health deteriorated rapidly, so I knew I needed to have a few important questions answered by him. My questions had been stored for almost 40 years and I wasn't sure that I would ever have a chance to ask him about them. Finally, a couple of months before he died, I had a chance to talk to him, one-on-one, about those long-unanswered questions.

I started by asking my father about the relationship between him and my grandfather, Walter Holden, from Pelham, Georgia. I remember spending time with my grandfather as a young kid while he was residing in Fort Valley, but couldn't put my father and grandfather in the same room, same city, or even the same state. My father was very hesitant about answering my questions, so I asked this question and immediately went into listening mode. My father thought carefully and answered me, partially, stating that he only saw my grandfather once in his life. He went on to brag about how drunk they got on the one time that they were together. I am not sure if that was the answer I needed, wanted, or expected, but it was certainly God's honest truth. It was clear that my father never had a father figure in his life, therefore he'd chosen to take the unpopular option of abandoning five kids and a young wife, for 13 years. Those were challenging years but they were what they were.

My mother, Hattie Hill Holden, is certainly one of the strongest women I have ever known. My mother considers herself a plain country girl from Roberta, Georgia. Roberta is a small neighboring city to Fort Valley and had a population of almost 920 citizens in the 1980s. That plain country girl raised five kids on her own and survived many challenges and struggles. Our family lived and bounced between three relatives, my grandmother, my aunt at her house in Roberta, and our faithful cousin, the late Mrs. Gaynelle Clark. After many moves between relatives, we were given an apartment with the Fort Valley Housing Authority in a great neighborhood called The Projects or Brick City. I must thank the late Claybon Edwards (First African American City Councilman in Fort Valley in 1970) and Rudolf J. Carson (First African American Mayor of Fort Valley in 1980) for encouraging the director at the housing authority to give an apartment to my mother. We needed that apartment in the projects so my oldest sister, Tawanna, could start kindergarten in the Peach County School system. Although we didn't have any furniture for the apartment, it felt like we had just moved into our mansion. It was a three-bedroom apartment with one room for the boys, another room for the girls, and the third room was for Momma. We even had one whole bathroom in the apartment with a shower tub combination installed by my mother's boyfriend who I consider a stepdad and a father figure, the late Tommy

L. Yates. Life was good and we were happy in our home in the Projects, and my mother remained in the community for 24 years.

The time we spent in the Project Community created a sense of community fellowship and friendship. Every family was a low-income earning family, all the kids had free lunch at school, and everyone was always welcome to visit without a formal dinner request. Some of the neighborly visits were to borrow items like sugar, milk, and cigarettes, and all we had to do was walk to the neighbor's house and we were welcomed.

In Fort Valley, we developed sports teams to compete with the other low-income communities in the city for bragging rights. The main sports were football, basketball, softball, boxing, and sometimes, plain ole street fighting. The winners of each event were only considered "Champions" at that moment. There could be a challenger for the following week so being a champion could be a short-term title. Unfortunately, some of the best athletes in the community and the city didn't have the discipline to remain in high school to compete on the collegiate level. Although the athletic talents were well-known in the community, chances to compete at the collegiate level were very slim. Then there were the athletes from Fort Valley that were just beasts at a sport that eventually had them playing at the professional level, like JaQuez Green, Marcus Robinson, DeMarcus Robinson, Tim Watson, Greg Lloyd, Danny Lockett, and Jimmy Reed.

My gift was to keep things straight academically in high school and pray that all my family members survived the struggles of a small town. Such struggles included the use of many types of drugs and alcohol, and experimenting with new drugs on the market, which has destroyed many Black communities and families. Drug and alcohol abuse also took control of my father and sister, Sherenette. It certainly wasn't easy to avoid the bumpy roads of life and they were challenging times, growing up in the hood.

My siblings were always near and dear to my heart, even though all five kids took a different direction in life. My three sisters were loving, but each had an isolated, individual personality. Tawanna, the oldest of the Holden bunch, has remained in Fort Valley and Warner Robins, Georgia all her life. She became the mother of four kids and is presently the grandmother of four. Sherenette, the real athlete of the bunch, was talented as a youth basketball and softball player. Although Sherenette was very athletic, she was the first kid in the family to be exposed to street drugs and declared to be possibly bisexual or gay. Knowing that my sister had declared herself to be a lesbian was heartbreaking news in the 1980s. At that time, I just couldn't understand the gay movement and how it had captured my sister. Lesbian Gay Bi-Sexual Transgender (LGBT) was not acknowledged and recognized in the 1980s and 1990s in Fort Valley, Georgia. Sherenette went on to have two kids but she died on my birthday in the year 2000 from a drug overdose. Rest in peace, my dear sister, we love you. My baby sister, Michelle Holden Hammonds, has a lot of the characteristics of our mother, as a young adult. She is hot-tempered and will fly off the handle at the smallest things, make that anything. Although she has a beautiful family, I pray for her to find God and maintain a calm temper in all the days of her life. Please pray for peace. I have always prayed for love, peace, and happiness for my entire family.

TWINS ARE TWINS FOREVER

My awesome twin brother, Hal Holden, is the star of the family. In my hometown, Hal is probably the most popular Holden of the bunch. Hal is 30 minutes older than me but sometimes he seems 10 years older. In the 80s and 90s, Hal had a very rough life as he started off being a small-town drug dealer and was in and out of jail many times. He is a very loving guy, but he can flip the switch within minutes/seconds; another hot-headed family member that has been through the test and is still hanging tough. Hal has taken the family through the challenges of supporting one's child or sibling. Most people in our hometown know Hal by the nickname of "Sugarmeat." I am not sure how the nickname came about but our hometown has a nickname for everyone.

BROTHERS IN CHRIST

I believe in the journey of life. God will add people to your inner circle to keep you on track for things and events that happen to you along the way. Those long-time friends are Marvin Walton, William Jones, Steve Thomas, Bryan Myers, Jeff Evans, and Johnny Thompson. These guys have been an inspiration and are all like brothers to me. I appreciate their friendship, love, guidance, knowledge, and listening ears throughout the years. I am my brothers' keeper.

AN EYE-OPENING EXPERIENCE

My high school sweetheart was Fran Risby, a sweet young lady from a deeply religious, church-going family. Fran's mother and father were both working full-time and were considered well-to-do in our hometown. It was an eye-opening experience when Fran's mother thought I wasn't good enough to take her daughter to my senior prom. Those were a very tough few months as I faced the reality of not being good enough to take my girlfriend to my senior prom. Moments like that are heartbreaking but they also give you the eye of the tiger to prove that you are good enough to hang with the best of the best. I later saw my former girlfriend's mother after being in the Marine Corps for about 15 years, and she was certainly shocked to know that my first career was almost complete. She told me that she was immensely proud of me, although I am not sure if that compliment healed the wound that had been made many years earlier.

JOINING THE MARINE CORPS WITH FRIENDS

After completing my junior year of high school, I decided to join the Marine Corps Delayed Entry Program with seven other friends from Peach County High School. As a senior in high school, I explained to my mother that I didn't want to be a burden on her after I graduated. I didn't want her to worry about me when I knew that the actions of my sisters and brother were enough to keep her parenting skills in overdrive. My Marine friends all realized that our parents didn't have the funds for us to pursue a college education. I feel that it was a mature decision to enlist and prepared to depart to Marine Corps Boot Camp in Parris

Island, South Carolina. Although I was mentally prepared to enter boot camp along with my high school buddies at my side, God had a slightly different plan. I was diagnosed with strep throat during my high school graduation week and that delayed me for about a week so I was behind all seven of my Marine buddies. On my departure day, it was like I was attending my funeral as I witnessed the tears shed by my mother and sisters, however, I was taking the first step towards becoming a man. It was tough for me, but I knew I had to do it. There was no turning back at this point, just full speed ahead. I prayed and hoped that God would continue to watch over my family in Fort Valley, and me, for the rest of my life. Surprisingly, when I headed to Parris Island for the Marine Corps Boot Camp, it was my first time leaving the state of Georgia.

Entering the Marine Corps was another eye-opening experience and certainly different from life in my hometown. The mental and physical demands and challenges of the Marine Corps will certainly separate the men from the boys. I thought it was going to be a walk in the park and that I'd be on cruise control after boot camp. That was certainly not the case. Everything in the Marine Corps was earned, not given. There was a different challenge at every rank that I earned, from Private First Class to Master Sergeant. I graduated from Parris Island without one family member present to see my moment of glory, however, I understood that no one in my family had the funds to travel 210 miles to see me graduate and earn the title of United States Marine. God was there with me and I thank you, God.

After boot camp, I was assigned to my military occupational specialty school in Twentynine Palms, California. Marine Base Twentynine Palms is located in the Mojave Desert, just outside of Palm Springs. I thought it was a blessing to travel to California from Fort Valley. Life was about to become over the top. At that point, I thought I was the luckiest Marine ever. However, California was where I started to enjoy the taste of alcohol. That's right, it was beer and alcohol almost daily after working hours, and certainly on weekends that I wasn't on military duty.

Traveling to the cities of Los Angeles, Venice Beach, Hollywood, Long Beach, and San Bernardino were all part of the travel and party plan. I remember contemplating buying a VIP pass to Zelda's Nightclub in Palm Springs because I was almost certain to visit the nightclub on Wednesday nights which was Ladies' Night and on Friday and Saturday night. I was thinking that I would love to be stationed in California for my career even though I had a special love for the east coast.

After completing my assignment at Twentynine Palms, I was assigned to the ultimate warfighting base for Marines at Camp Lejeune in North Carolina. The 8th Marine Regiment and subordinate units seemed to always be on standby to travel to a war zone or relief effort under the command of the Commander-in-Chief. It was a shock to go from being a Zelda's Nightclub VIP cardholder in California to checking out my weapon and war gear at the 8th Marine Regiment. The Marine Corps Air Station in New River, North Carolina had a nice, enlisted nightclub that was a weekend relief place for most Marines in the area. After one year, I was glad to be ordered to report to Okinawa, Japan for duty. What a relief! My mind was too immature to report to a warzone because I was more interested in travel, adventure, and partying. Life was soon about to take a major change in direction.

LIVING IN JAPAN

Okinawa, Japan was another delightful duty station for a young Marine. The weather was great most of the time except for during the typhoon season. There were a good number of Marines and military guys that married the local Japanese women. I didn't think my mother would approve of a daughter-in-law from another country so marrying a Japanese woman was not in my long-term plan.

The Japanese audio technology for music was by far the best in the world at that time. It was on Okinawa that I, like most Marines overseas, paid about $2,000 for a seven-layer piece of stereo equipment with about 2,000-watt speakers that could run entertainment at most nightclubs. Purchasing quality stereo equipment was a hobby and it was a way of life in Japan. Okinawa City and Naha were the nightlife highlights for the island. While on Okinawa, I also traveled to Seoul, South Korea for major warfighting exercises called Team Spirit and Bearhunt. The memories of both cities will be cherished for a lifetime. After a year of being on the island, it was time to move to the Marine Corps Air Station in Cherry Point, North Carolina.

Cherry Point, North Carolina was the first duty station that forced me to make some career decisions that would help me to mature. Cherry Point helped me to focus on my quality of life, establishing a family, and a solid military career. Upon arrival, I was assigned to work with three hardcore Marines that were focused on career advancement and making the Marine Corps a way of life. My focus, after being in the Marine Corps for three years, was on how many clubs and how many women I could date while living a lackadaisical lifestyle. The three guys that turned my life around at that time were Staff Sergeant Robert Green, Sergeant Michael Gray, and Sergeant Bryan Myers. They were all in great physical shape and were serious about their military business. I had to shape up mentally and get my mind right to keep up the pace with these fellows. I knew that being a workhorse was in me from the days of picking peaches in Fort Valley, but these guys bought their "A" game each day of the week. We worked at a 24-hour communications facility, so the work hours rotated, and the need to perform without mistakes was the standard set by Staff Sergeant Robert Green. He was a star-studded Marine boss that took me under his wing and showed me what military leadership was all about. He was my first father figure after joining the Marine Corps, where there was a demand for winning at all costs and on multiple levels. Second place was the first loser in his thought process. I was competing to be promoted to the rank of Corporal and my Staff Sergeant provided some crystal clear guidance. The guidance he gave me was that I needed to win first place, or he would personally have the second promotion removed from consideration. He reminded me that 10 sharp Marines were competing for two promotion-allocated slots. I was thinking that it was great that first or second place would earn me a promotion to the next rank. He told me that my objective was to be selected as the number one candidate. They were tough competition, but I was selected for the number one position. That promotion process was quite stressful but most meritorious promotions are for the stellar Marines, and not for the everyday military member. At this point in my life, I started thinking like a champion.

MY NEW LIFE - A YOUNG MARRIAGE AND STARTING A FAMILY

Although I thought I was having the time of my military life, it was about to change drastically. In 1987, I was about to change my outlook and added more weight to my shoulders. I was dating Rosemary (Rose) Raines, a senior at my old high school in Peach County. I appreciated the recommendation to date me from Gayle Raines who was Rose's oldest sister. We probably wouldn't be together today if it weren't for that sisterly recommendation. Initially, my family didn't approve of the relationship and I have no idea why. Rose was a sweet young lady with a heart of gold. She came from a family of 12 siblings, comprised of nine brothers and three sisters. Of course, my initial idea of marriage was unlimited sex without having to jump through a lot of hurdles. I was 21 years old and sweet little Rose was 17 at the time of our marriage. I promised Rose's mother that I would take care of her and I have kept my word for over 33 years.

We were married by the Justice of the Peace in New Bern, North Carolina. I needed to borrow $20 from my roommate to purchase the marriage license. We knew that we weren't prepared for marriage, but our lives were totally in God's hands. We also didn't have an apartment to live in until after I had earned a few military paydays. That is what you call starting at the bottom, with literally a few dollars. My best friend and

Marine buddy in North Carolina, Marvin Walton, had a fancy low-income trailer outside of Camp Lejeune with an extra bedroom, and that was the spot that I needed Rose to live in while I got my crap together. It was not the ideal setup, but I needed help to have a decent start for my marriage.

Blessings started coming my way after we were married, and we found out shortly after, that Rose was pregnant. Yes, life just got real at that point. Rose was really scared to share the news about being pregnant, so I shared the news with our family in a joking manner. I was always the person that looked at the glass as being half full. I have always relied on blessings from God to take us through the good times and the bad.

On September 3, 1988, Marcus Anthony Holden was born at the Marine Base Cherry Point Hospital in North Carolina. A healthy baby boy is just what I wanted on our first try. Marcus Holden was here to stay so that added more weight on my shoulders. At that point, there were two people in the world that I was responsible for, which meant that I was needed to re-enlist for four more years and was well on my way to being a career Marine with a family.

Shortly after my son was born, I was given orders to report to Okinawa, Japan for a one-year assignment without the family. Our joint decision was to move the family from Fort Valley until my unaccompanied assignment was complete. Moving back in with your parents is not always the best decision if you have other options. The year was filled with challenges for both of our families. It was an uncomfortable situation that I felt much better about when the tour was over. We felt that our decision to relocate Rose and Marcus to Georgia for the year would be a good one but that was not the case. You live and learn. The good thing about that year was that it was time for Marcus to learn to walk and get to know his grandparents. Rose's father took Marcus under his wing as he did with all his grandkids. A special bond formed between Marcus and his grandfather during that year that I was overseas.

The second year in Japan went by quickly from my perspective. Before I knew it, I was headed back to Camp Lejeune to be with my family. I reported to Camp Lejeune in 1989, not knowing that it would be a few months before I went to war. I thought I would be settled until Saddam Hussein from Iraq invaded the nation of Kuwait. I knew the chances of going to war were high when the invasion was reported on CNN News.

On December 10, 1990, I was one of 24,000 thousand Marines standing in formation, preparing to head to the Middle East. You know it's a big deal when you are on the front page of the New York Post newspaper. I think it was the largest gathering of Marines in history and I was there. The Commandant of the Marine Corps spoke to the Marine warfighters and told us that the President of the United States needed us to provide support in the Middle East. In layman's terms, we were going to war very soon.

Desert Shield/Desert Storm was a display of American aviation superiority never seen before. The enemy forces were worn down, tired, hungry, and lost, with no will to fight. The allied forces simply demolished the normal Iraqi military and the supposedly elite Iraqi Republican Guard forces. I worked at the Marine Forces Headquarters in Saudi Arabia under Lieutenant General Walter Boomer. After returning from Desert Shield/Desert Storm, I did not rest well for about a year. I wanted to fight, kill, and support my country but a heavy mental price is paid when involved with a dangerous war effort. My mother, wife, and son mentioned that I was not mentally stable upon returning to the United States, however, I'm glad that the nightmares, bad dreams, and demons eventually disappeared.

I was assigned to the Marine Corps Recruiting School in San Diego in 1992. This was another assignment that I didn't want. I was sure I was going to be selected for Marine Corps Drill Instructor duty at Parris Island where east coast Marines are trained during boot camp. However, the decision to become a Marine Corps Recruiter was not up for negotiation and therefore I went on to attend the formal training school for Marine Recruiters.

Recruiting School in San Diego was relaxed and very enjoyable. The stress occurred when I became a canvassing recruiter in Lancaster County (Amish Country), Pennsylvania. I was awarded the prestigious Recruiter Centurion Award for recruiting over 100 people to join the Marine Corps. Recruiting young high school kids was a great assignment and it was quite stressful to make the numbers required to complete Recruit Training. This was an independent duty in the streets, daily, and I loved it. Winning Rookie Recruiter of the Year for the region was all good while it lasted. I considered becoming a Career Recruiter, but a special assignment was presented for duty at Headquarters Marine Corps in Arlington, Virginia.

REPORTING TO HEADQUARTERS MARINE CORPS AND THE PENTAGON

Receiving orders to report for duty at Headquarters Marine Corps was a special blessing that was not in my plan but clearly, was part of God's plan. Melvin Dove, a Marine that previously worked for me, recommended that I chat with the Senior Enlisted Advisor about an assignment in the Washington, DC area. Master Sergeant Ronald Ginyard and I chatted and I was selected for the position. As they say, most times it's who you know when it comes to obtaining a high-profile position with Headquarters Marine Corps in the DC area. Let me be clear that all military commands in the Washington, DC area are well-oiled corporate headquarters. Sometimes you need to remind yourself that you are still in the military. Providing guidance and support to the Fleet Marine Corps units was not an easy task. The duty was incredibly stressful every day. I was also selected to serve with the military's highest uniform command – the Joint Chiefs of Staff. The Joint Chiefs of Staff is the body of the most senior uniformed leaders within the United States Department of Defense, which advise the President of the United States, the Secretary of Defense, the Homeland Security Council, and the National Security Council on military matters. It was amazing to work at the Pentagon with approximately 28,000 military and civilian employees in the world's largest office building. There have been many military members that have served as Sergeants, Navy Petty Officers, Army Captains, and even Navy Admirals but very few were assigned to work in the military highest uniform command. Thanks to all those military members from Fort Valley that have served faithfully and supported our nation. My hometown has only about 9,000 citizens, so this was amazing.

After the tour of duty at Headquarters Marine Corps and the Pentagon, I was assigned to report to Kaneohe Bay, Hawaii. Life was very relaxed in Hawaii and it was a great place to be a military member. The weather was great, the nightlife was exceptionally good, and it was a great place to get in good physical shape. As the senior enlisted adviser of the Marine Corps Base Kaneohe Bay Communications Center, we were awarded the Defense Message System Facility of the Year for two consecutive years. It was known as the worst facility when I arrived and the best by the time I departed for my next military command. With God's blessings, on September 11, 2001, I was stationed at Kaneohe Bay when the awful terror attacks happened. That was a day that many of us will never forget. My mission in Hawaii was complete. Life was great and I thought I was on top of the world.

I reported back to the Headquarters Marine Corps in 2002 for my twilight tour. I was challenged by my new Civilian Director of Information Technology to bring the Facility of the Year award to Headquarters. It was not an easy task and was surrounded by a lot of negative moving parts. My Marines were out of control, disrespectful, and undisciplined, upon arrival. The need to succeed was one of my greatest challenges. The region was still under heavy stress after the awful terror attacks on the Pentagon, New York Trade Center, and Shanksville, PA. We lost a lot of great Americans on that tragic day. The military was back at war, and things had changed a great deal for all Americans. This war had a few different names such as Operation Enduring Freedom, Operation Iraqi Freedom, and Operation New Dawn.

Supporting the war from the Pentagon wasn't an easy task, but it had to be done.

I stayed focused on the tasks at hand, and we were awarded the Facility of the Year award in 2003 and 2004. The award was great, but the days were exceptionally long and stressful, with a few internal antagonists trying to damage my will and reputation, to win. I found myself under investigation by the Inspector General's office. Painfully, I endured a full-scope investigation that ended with no finding whatsoever, but I was mentally tired and knew that my military days would soon come to an end. I decided to retire as a Marine Corps Master Sergeant and laid my uniform to rest in June of 2005.

It was a great tour of duty and 21 years of faithful and dedicated military service. My retirement officer at Headquarters Marine Corps was my awesome cousin, Rear Admiral Alvin Holsey, currently still supporting Navy operations for the United States. Please continue to pray for all military members that have served and those members currently fighting for our freedom as Americans.

LIFE AFTER THE MARINE CORPS

Rose, Marcus, and I packed the household and moved to McDonough, Georgia to start our new post-military experience. Life after the Marine Corps has taken a smooth sailing approach. God has again blessed my family with peace, love, and happiness while creating many testimonies in various areas. We have enjoyed visiting Washington, DC for the initial inauguration of President Barack Obama, the opening of the Dr. Martin Luther King Jr. memorial, and the opening of The Smithsonian National

Museum of African American History and Culture. We are proud and active members of the Shiloh Baptist Church in McDonough. I have been working as a human resources corporate recruiter for 15 years with approximately 7,000 candidate hires. We have a loving granddaughter, Makiah Juliette Holden.

That is how I went from the Projects to the Pentagon and then back to the great state of Georgia.

We give all the honor and praise to our almighty God for watching over us through the years. Life has taken me from the Projects to the lakeside for 54 years and counting. Life will hit you many times, knock you down, and sometimes appear to knock you out. However, I encourage you to lean on almighty God to always get you through tough and challenging times. He will make a way out of no way. I am a living witness of what God can and will do.

I would like to thank my wife of 33 years and counting, the lovely Rose Holden, for having faith and hope in God and for helping me to take care of our precious family. I promised my mother-in-law (Hattie B. Raines) that I would take care of you, and I think I have been a man of my word. And Still Champion.

ABOUT
HAROLD HOLDEN

Harold Holden was born on May 3, 1966, in Fort Valley, Georgia. Fort Valley is known for the largest peach production in the Peach State of Georgia. A graduate of Peach County High School, Harold was employed in his teenage years as a peach picker and a residential construction helper to help his struggling single mother support her family of five children.

After graduating high school in 1984, Harold enlisted in the Marine Corps. Harold's Marine Corps career highlights included a tour of duty at the Pentagon, assigned to the Military Joint Staff. Harold also served in Desert Shield/Desert Storm as a Communications Center Sergeant. Other military assignments included Headquarters Marine Corps in Hawaii, Camp Lejeune in North Carolina, and Okinawa, Japan. Harold's special assignment included a tour of duty as a military recruiter in Lancaster, Pennsylvania - Amish Country. Harold retired as a highly decorated Marine Corps Master Sergeant (E8) with 21 years of dedicated, honest, and faithful service.

Harold has been employed as a corporate level recruiter for 15 years with over 6,000 candidate hires to his credit. He is also an assistant ministry leader and active member at Shiloh Baptist Church in McDonough, GA.

Harold married the lovely Rose (Raines) Holden in 1987 and their son, Marcus A. Holden, was born in 1988. He has given his parents one awesome grandchild, Makiah Holden. God has richly blessed Harold's family throughout the years.

ROADBLOCKS TO MY DESTINY

by Mitchell Mormon

*Roadblock: something that blocks progress or
prevents accomplishment of an objective.
~ Merriam-Webster Dictionary*

ROADBLOCK #1 - USED AND ABUSED SEXUALLY

They say all things work together for good to those who love
God and are called according to his purpose. On this journey
called life, I have learned that we all face roadblocks to our
destiny in life. For me, the first roadblock occurred when I was
six years old, living in Williamsburg, Virginia, during my first
summer out of school. My mom and dad both worked during
the day so that they could be home at night. They had recently
moved into a new area and my parents didn't know much
about the people in the community, so finding a good sitter for
me and my two siblings was, to say the least, a challenge for
them. They didn't know who would be a good sitter, but they
eventually found one.

I was the oldest child. Our first sitter was young, 17 or 18
years old, and she would watch us during the summer. She

would come to our house from 10:00 a.m. to 4:00 or 5:00 p.m., Monday through Friday. Everything was great for a while. She came in and fed us breakfast and lunch, and at certain times during the day, she would send us outside to play. However, on one particular day when my siblings and I were about to go outside, she sent my siblings outside to play and told me that I had to go and take a nap so that my brother and sister would see that we all had to start taking a nap before our parents got home from work. So, I went into my bedroom and laid on the bed to take a nap. After about 15 minutes, just as I was about to doze off to sleep, the sitter came into the bedroom. I thought she was coming to check on me, but she had other plans. She told me to slide over so that she could lay down with me and take a nap too. Shortly after she laid down beside me, I felt her hand fondling my private parts, and I didn't know what to do. She was touching my penis, and even though I was a young boy, I was aroused and my penis became hard. The sitter then pulled me on top of her and placed my penis inside her vagina. I wasn't exactly sure what was going on, but she knew what she was doing, and after it was over, she got up and told me to get dressed and go outside to play with my siblings.

Little did I know at that point that pre-mature sexual exposure was the first trap or roadblock that the enemy had set for me. That evening when my mother got home, I told her what the sitter had done, and she fired her. Life went on and my mother didn't talk about it with me anymore, and although I didn't understand why the sitter would do this with me, I didn't bring it up either. Eventually, my parents would get another sitter.

This time, my mother got an older sitter for us who was about 25 years old. She seemed to be pretty cool. We had the same routine every day and everything seemed to be going great. However, one day the sitter sent my sister next door to play with the neighbors' daughter and she asked me and my younger brother to go into the living room and lay on the floor, so we did what she told us to do. Once we were both on the floor looking up at the ceiling, the sitter came into the living room and stood over me and my brother so that we were looking between her legs. My brother and I looked at each other with a questionable look on our faces, both wondering what she was doing. We didn't have to wonder for long. She told us to take turns putting our fingers inside her panties and to play with her until her panties were wet, and then she would tell us to stop. This became a routine for us for a while. My brother and I were baffled as to why someone who was old enough to be our mother was doing this, but one day at the end of the summer, out of the blue, this sitter quit and never came back. I started to feel used and abused and wondered what was wrong with me that made girls do that stuff to me. Although I was young, I knew that something wasn't right.

My dad left us, and with me being the oldest, my mother was counting on me to help out with the things that needed to be done in the house, including washing the dishes, doing laundry, and watching my siblings, so I pushed these incidents out of my mind. I had to help my family.

After my dad left, Mom couldn't afford to stay in the home we lived in, with only her salary, so we had to move to a less expensive home. We eventually moved into a box house with four rooms. There was no bathroom but there was an outhouse that we had to use. We took baths in a large foot tub, where we would have to heat water on the stove, and my brother and I would have to bathe in the same water. Our sister would get a fresh tub of water to bathe in. There were no doors in the house, so Mom put up curtains to separate the kitchen and living room. We lived in that little box house for a while and one day Mom came home and told us she found an apartment. It was toward the end of the school year, so I asked my mom if we could stay one more month so that I could work in my cousin's field and earn a few dollars to buy school supplies for the next school year. She said we could stay for one more month.

During that month, I worked in the field picking butter beans, string beans, and potatoes, all for $5 a bushel. By the end of the month, I had earned enough money to buy my school supplies for the next school year which made me feel good because I was contributing and helping my mom. When the month was almost over, we started to get excited and began packing the few clothes we had. The apartment we moved into looked like a new 3-bedroom apartment; it was a two-story unit with an upstairs and downstairs.

By this time, I was 11 years old and in the 6th grade. My brother and I shared a bedroom, our sister had her bedroom, and of course, Mom had her room. We had a full bathroom, and although we were living in the projects, to us it was home, and the people were friendly. At least we didn't have to go outside to use the bathroom. We thought we had moved up in life. As we settled into our new home, we made new friends and things were going great.

One night, my brother and I went downstairs to get some water and were surprised when we turned on the kitchen light and saw something we'd never seen before...roaches. We were scared out of our wits because we had never seen roaches before, so we got our water and ran back upstairs. We had to take the bitter with the sweet. The next day, we told our mom and she contacted the rental office to have an exterminator come to spray for the roaches.

We lived in that apartment for about six years. My life was looking up, I had nice friends to play with every day, and I learned a few skills. I became a newspaper boy and delivered papers to almost 70 customers each day, seven days a week. I also acquired upholstery skills, working in an upholstery shop, upholstering everything from school bus seats to antique living room furniture. I felt good because I was helping my mom.

I was in the 11th grade when one day, after getting off the school bus, I walked to our apartment and saw a note on the door. It was an eviction letter that read, "You are being evicted. You have 30 days to move out of this apartment and turn in the keys." I was upset, devastated, and ashamed, at the same time. When Mom came home, I showed her the note, and being the strong woman that she was, all she said was, "We have to find somewhere else to live son." I said, "Ok Mom, but where will we go?" She said she didn't know yet, but she would find somewhere for us to live. It was the end of the school year and I was going to be a senior, moving to a new school. We moved to a two-bedroom house that was near my mom's family. Mom had her room and my brother and I shared a bedroom. The house had a closed-in porch that we turned into a bedroom for my sister.

ROADBLOCK #2 – DRUGS AND ALCOHOL

Since we were near family, things were not too bad. I attended the local school in that area as a senior, which was challenging because I didn't know anyone at the new school, but I tried to fit it in. The school was predominantly white, and out of our class of 97 students, 17 were Black. I tried to fit in with those 17 classmates, so of course, I had to do what they did. Most of them played sports so I played football, and started drinking and smoking grass because that's what they did. Drugs and alcohol became another roadblock laid by the enemy. When trying to fit in and be accepted, people do things they wouldn't normally do, or they use drugs and alcohol as a way to numb their feelings and forget the bad things they don't want to remember. For me, it was the pre-exposure to sex at a young age that I had never dealt with.

After two years, the landlord decided to sell the house and we had to move again. We ended up in another apartment, this time, a three-bedroom. I thanked God for that because it got me away from the crowd who introduced me to drugs and alcohol, at least for a while.

When I was 19, I decided to move into my own place, but to do that I needed a job. Being responsible for paying rent, electric and water bills, food, and furniture required a steady income. I was looking in the newspaper one day and saw an ad for a warehouse worker with no experience needed. I thought that I could get that job so I went to the warehouse, got the job, and started working the next day.

On my first day on the job, I was required to assist the maintenance guy with the welding together of a couple of metal strips. He gave me a pair of dark eye protection glasses and we began to weld. This was exciting because I'd never seen anything like it before. We ate lunch and resumed welding. At the end of the day, I was so happy to have learned and experienced something I had never done before. That night after dinner and a nice hot shower, I sat down to watch a little TV, and after a while, began to wipe my eyes. It felt as if something was in my eyes but the more I wiped them, the more they burned and itched. It wasn't long before I was barely able to see a glimpse out of my eyes. I knew something was wrong, so I made my way to my neighbor's apartment (a friend of the family). After I told him how my eyes were feeling, we jetted to the emergency room where I was seen and treated for photokeratitis which is the burning of the cornea by ultraviolet rays. Although the pain was severe, I thanked God that the damage to my eyes wasn't permanent. The doctor put some eye drops in my eyes and covered both with eye patches. My friend took me back home and since I couldn't see anything, I decided to go to bed because the patches had to stay on for 48 hours. My friend called my mother for me and she came over and took care of me until I was well. Thank God for moms!

Because of the damage to my eyes, I eventually ended up moving back home with my mom as I could no longer work. One day I was sitting out on the sidewalk on the curb near our home, trying to figure out where my life was going, when I looked up the street and saw a familiar car driving up. It was an ex-coworker that I had kept in contact with who I referred to as my little sister. She got out of her car and said, "Big Brah, let's go into the Army." I guessed she could tell by the look on my face that I needed more information about the Army, so she gave me the lowdown about how we could join the Army under the buddy system program, and how we would be stationed together so we could encourage each other, especially during boot camp. Well, that's what we did, we joined the Army. Little did we know that because we had chosen different career fields or Military Occupational Specialties (MOS), our start dates for training were different, so needless to say, I felt as if I'd been hoodwinked. That was in July of 1979 and to this day in 2020, I have still not seen my little sis!

I went to Fort Jackson, South Carolina for Basic Training and Advanced Individual Training (AIT). After AIT, I received my Permanent Change of Station (PCS) orders and was off to Germany, a place I had never been to before, with a new culture, new food, and new people. What intrigued me the most was that there was no speed limit on the autobahns (highways). I lived in the Army barracks which amounted to a room for two soldiers to share, and that took some time to get used to. I got settled into my room and my roommate looked somewhat like me, light-skinned and tall, and we both had waves in our hair. We became close and always had each other's back, covering for each other, and sharing information about the military and life. However, although we were close, I couldn't share my pre-sexual experiences with him. I couldn't share that with anyone because I was too embarrassed and ashamed to even talk about it.

One day while I was going to work, I was introduced to my new supervisor and we went on to become good friends as well, after serving for 10 to12 months together, going to Physical Training (PT), and then to work. I had a good job working in Human Resources, and after work, I would go to my room to chill. One afternoon, I heard a knock on my door and it was my supervisor. I didn't know if I was in trouble or not. After I let him in my room, my supervisor asked me if I wanted a car, and I was like, "Yes, sir," so he threw me a set of keys. We went outside to look at the car, and I smiled from ear to ear with joy in my heart because I'd been given a car. I thought that things couldn't get any better. When I got in the car and sat down, to my surprise, the car was a stick shift with gears and an extra pedal to the left of the brake. My eyes widened and my supervisor asked, "What's wrong?" I replied that I had never driven a stick shift car in my life. My supervisor laughed and said not to worry as he would teach me how to drive a stick. Sometimes, life comes at you fast and you must always be ready for the good and the bad. These two rounds of life hit me with a one-two punch and a left hook that knocked me down, but I got up because I was about to encounter another unexpected life experience.

My supervisor and another friend went for a ride to a town called Frankfurt in Germany. I went along for the ride, but little did I know that the territory we were entering was known for buying and selling drugs. The person driving the car I was in, stopped the car and said, "Man, the police are behind us." The Polizei (police) came up on the passenger side of the car which was the side I was on, and the officer quickly opened the car door. He had the biggest gun I had ever seen, aimed at my head. I was so afraid that I froze in my seat as the police officer continued to reach for my friend's throat with his other hand, while still holding the gun, but it was too late, my friend had just swallowed the drugs he bought. I knew nothing about what my friend had done but knew that if he had been caught with the drugs, he would have been in trouble. However, since there was no evidence, the police let us go. My friend drove us back to the barracks, fast. Thinking back on it, I realized that I could have been gone if that gun had gone off by accident. However, another plot by the enemy was spoiled because God had kept me safe again. He knew he had work for me to do. I didn't know it at the time, but I found out later that my grandmother had been praying for me.

The next weekend, I decided to change my circle and hang out with another friend, who was married with two children. I figured it would be a bit safer, especially when went go out. My friend picked me up from the barracks and took me to meet his wife and two children, a beautiful family I hoped to one day emulate. We sat down in his living room and he handed me a German beer (Frankenbier) that was 15-19% alcohol, compared to the beer from America which was 5-7% alcohol. His wife fixed a little food, and we ate and had another beer. My friend asked if I was ready to go back to the barracks and I said yes. He then let me know that he had been drinking all day.

Later that day, as we left his house, my friend grabbed another 8-pack of beer and put it in the back seat of the car. We rode in my friend's Volkswagen Beetle and as we got closer to the barracks, we both decided to have another beer. As we approached the light at a busy intersection, my friend thought he could make it through the light. Well, we got halfway through and were hit by another car trying to make it through the same light. The impact of the accident caused both our heads to hit the windshield. I don't remember if we had our seatbelts on or not, but I could feel blood running down my face. I had a cut on my head and was a little dizzy, but the only thing I could think of was to get rid of the beer before the police arrived on the scene, because it would mean automatic jail time for that type of violation. My friend asked me if I was alright and I said yeah. However, when I looked back at my friend, I could see his head leaning back on the car seat and the right side of his face was cut half-open. I told him that we had to get him to the hospital ASAP. My friend had so much alcohol in him that he didn't feel anything. I guess that was a good thing at that moment as at least he couldn't feel the pain. It was a bloody sight, but we made it to the hospital by ambulance.

That was another roadblock the enemy used to try and take me out again, but God stepped in once again and said no. Even though I was out there doing my own thing, I knew my grandmother had to be praying for me. When I look back over my life now, I can see the hand of God on my life, keeping me safe for a greater calling in life. It was June of 1982, and I would soon depart Germany for another PCS assignment in the United States.

I was finally back in the United States of America but could tell right away, that things had changed. The speed limit, music, food, and of course, the nightclubs were different. I had always been a people person and was told that I had never met a stranger, so it was easy for me to make new friends. So, I decided to jump right back into the party life with my new friends who were into smoking marijuana. Of course, being in the US Army and smoking marijuana, was not a good mix.

Although I was scared, I tried it anyway because everyone else was doing it. I knew that if I were to be "hot" during a urinalysis test, my career would be over and I'd receive a dishonorable discharge from the service. I did not want that. The Army had been good to me. I was getting paid every 14 days, had a place to live, and was fed three meals a day. That was a beautiful thing. My life was good.

One night, a friend asked me to go to the NCO club which was on the military base. We went to the club and partied for a while and then decided to go off base to another club. After partying for a while, my friend handed me a small package that had a price on it. I accepted the package and it was cocaine. After that night, I began snorting cocaine regularly and didn't think twice about the consequences. All I knew was I was having a good time, until one Sunday when I woke up and just about all my money was gone. I shook my head, and could not believe that I had spent that much money on drugs. Although I had a good time, I had nothing to show for my money.

Later on that day, my friend knocked on my barracks door and asked me how I was doing. I shared with him how I was feeling...all my money was gone and I felt terrible. My friend said, "I feel you, man. Let's slow down." I could not have been happier to hear those words slow down.

VICTORY - WALKING IN HIS PLAN AND PURPOSE

It was a cool, winter Sunday morning when suddenly, I looked out the window and saw two young ladies walking together toward the barracks. I thought, WOW! My eyes were stuck on one young lady in particular, as she was talking out loud, and her friend said, "Oh yeah, those are the two new soldiers that processed in the unit on Friday." Her friend suggested that they introduce themselves and ask those two new young soldiers to go out on a date.

On Monday morning, we had Physical Training (PT) and afterward, I went off to work in the office. I was the Supply Non-Commissioned Officer for the unit, and also called cadence during PT. On this particular morning, I went to the First Sergeant's office in the Orderly Room to order supplies for my unit and as I was exiting the First Sergeant's office, I almost didn't recognize her because she was dressed differently, but it was the young lady I had been eyeing from my window. She was in the Orderly Room completing her in-processing into the unit, at 1st AG, The Big Red One. I spoke to her and she returned the greeting. There was something very special about her voice, it touched my heart as no other woman had before. The next day, I saw her at work and my heart beat quickly, and my mind was on her all day and all night. I said to myself, "Self, move slow, if she is for you, the time will come."

I called my grandmother and told her I was tired of running the streets and that I was ready to settle down. She told me she would pray that God would send me a wife. So, I waited 30 days before me and my friend asked the young ladies out on a date. The weekend came and they accepted our invitation. We took those young ladies out to the NCO Club and they had a good time, talking, dancing, and sipping on a few drinks. Afterward, we took them back to the barracks and called it a night, but I had already decided to ask her out for lunch the next day, and of course, she accepted.

I met her the next day at her job and asked if she was ready for lunch. It was our first lunch date, at the Army Dining Facility, and as we were eating, I was so excited to be having a conversation with her, that I got straight to the point and asked her a couple of questions. I told her what I was looking for in a woman and asked her if she could be that woman. Well, I liked her responses. I asked her if she had any questions for me and she did, and apparently, she liked my responses too. We decided to be a couple after that. Cupid's arrow had landed. My grandmother's prayers had been answered because we dated for about five months before I decided to ask her the big question. I kneeled on one knee, looked into her beautiful eyes, and asked, "Will you marry me?" She said yes and my heart was so full of joy! I had finally met my match, the woman who said she would tame me.

I married my soul mate on September 3rd, and a little over a year later, we had our first baby, a handsome boy. A year after that, I rededicated my life to the Lord. I was a backslider, who had given my life to the Lord during an R.W. Schambach tent revival when I was 10 years old. I had joined the youth choir at my church and sang on youth Sundays. The Word was instilled in me way back when I was a young child and now I realized why the enemy was out to steal and destroy my life. However, God's hands were upon me and nothing the enemy did could snatch me out of God's hands, not even because of the bad decisions I'd made.

During a visit to Virginia one Christmas, my wife encouraged me to talk to my dad about how I had felt since he had left when I was a young boy. Dad and I had that conversation and I told him how I felt and asked him why he had left, and why he never told my siblings and me that he loved us. My dad apologized to me and said that he didn't know how important that was for us because his dad had never told him that he loved him. After that, I forgave my dad and we had a better father and son relationship. God said, "He that finds a wife finds a good thing and obtains favor of the Lord." I had found my good thing.

Shortly after that, I received PCS orders for Germany, again. This time, I was going there while walking in the plan and purpose of God's calling on my life. I was assigned to an Army post in Bad Kissingen, where God would use me to serve in my local church, at the District and Jurisdictional level as a Deacon and Finance Chairman. This time around, I was on a different assignment. Instead of allowing the enemy to use me, I would walk in God's assignment, and during the almost 10 years we were in Europe, I was a witness for the Lord. I was instrumental in winning hundreds of souls for The Kingdom and in helping others answer the call of God on their life.

God is still blessing me and I'm still winning in life today. And just in case you are wondering about that gorgeous woman I asked to marry me, we are in this race together and have been married 37 years. Our marriage gets stronger every day. My wife and I are both licensed ministers, life coaches, and marriage counselors who serve faithfully through the Tabernacle of

Praise Church International, under the awesome leadership of Pastor TJ McBride.

I continue to fight the good fight of faith, knowing that he who begins a good work in God's name, can finish it until the day of redemption. As a man of God and a child of The King, I grow in faith, because I know victory is mine. I hope I have encouraged you with my story, and that you will keep fighting the good fight. Don't ever quit or give up. Know that God will never leave you or forsake you. He has a plan and purpose for your life. You may not understand it but trust the process...trust God. Don't stop fighting because, in the end, you will win! You are a CHAMPION.

ABOUT
MITCHELL MORMON

Mitchell J. Mormon was born and raised in the state of Virginia. He is an Advanced Medical Support Assistant for the Department of Veteran Affairs, a Certified Counselor, Life Coach, and a Licensed Minister with Tabernacle of Praise Church International, under the leadership of Pastor T.J. McBride. Mitchell is also a retired U. S. Army veteran who proudly served his country. While serving in the U. S. Army, Mitchell received many service ribbons and medals, however, the one he is most proud of is the Meritorious Service Medal which is the highest award given during peacetime.

Mitchell has had to face and conquer incredible challenges in his life, however, his faith and trust in God are what gave him the strength and power to overcome each of those challenges. As he grew in the faith, he realized that from each experience he gained wisdom and knowledge that would help him as a minister of the gospel, counselor, and life coach to assist others. What the devil meant for evil and to destroy him, he has used for nearly 25 years to successfully help others in conquering their challenges and fears so that they, too, walk in victory.

On September 3, 2020, Mitchell celebrated 37 years of marriage to his one and only wife and soul mate, Gloria Mormon. They are blessed with three splendid children and four beautiful grandchildren. Mitchell is looking forward to his second retirement in 2020.

Contact Mitchell at info@mitchandgloriamormon.com

IDENTITY CRISIS

by Jamal L. Burt

So, I heard I'm a polymath... but I don't like it. I just recently learned what the term polymath meant, and its meaning is a little daunting to me. I'm just a regular guy with a huge propensity for wearing my heart on my sleeve – to a fault. Yeah, I pay attention to many details, I remember much of what I am taught and what I learn, and I share what I've learned regularly. It seems to be what I was put here for. Though many may think this is a great ability, I don't see it as a big deal at all. Loving, caring, and encouraging relationships mean more to me, and finding them – that has been the greatest purpose of my life. Yet, it's hard to trust people when you see yourself as inadequate. Being academically gifted is not a big thing to someone who loves people; being shy and socially awkward makes loving people very hard...

My mom said I began reading when I was three years old. I would sit at the table with the newspaper and try to sound out words and decipher their meanings. When I didn't know a word, I'd ask my mom how to pronounce it, and I wouldn't forget it. Having a photographic memory helped. Picking things up very quickly never stopped me from asking a lot of questions, though.

"Mom, what's racism?"

Something I had no business asking, but I would anyway. Though I didn't realize it at the time, this thirst for accumulating and dispensing knowledge was going to be the cornerstone of my life and career.

Along with all of the things I received as a child, the most valued thing God graced me with was a capacity for knowledge. I loved learning. I read everything. I often remember going to my grandmother's house on the weekends, and when I got bored, I would sit in front of her bookcase filled with World Book Encyclopedias and read them. Whatever thought came into my head that I wanted to know, any term or concept I saw on TV that piqued my curiosity, or anything I overheard adults talk about that interested me, I looked it up. It was like surfing the net. Once I read about one topic, there was something in the entry that would pique my interest, and I would look that up next, and so on, and so on.

My parents were amazing. I was raised with a lot of love, comfort, and support. It was never a matter of having to struggle – my parents worked too hard for that. We were middle-class by most '80s standards. My sister and I never had what all the other kids had. Being middle-class meant we had money to live well enough, but I often had to wait for things other kids already had. I had to go over to some other kid's house to play with the toys I wanted to have. Yet, my parents did get us other stuff: piles of construction sets, from Legos to Construx and Erector sets, musical instruments, electronics for gaming, a drafting table, bikes. My parents spent money on things that would introduce us to a higher level of thinking – a higher level of experience. While other kids were asking for landscapes to play with their action figures, I spent hours in my room building my own. Everything centered around using my brain to solve problems. I couldn't get enough of puzzle books. I read everything my little eyes could see.

In addition to feeding an ever-growing intellect, I had a hunger for expression. Whether it be through the written word, art, or speaking, I always had the urge to take what was in my mind and try to explain it to people, somehow. There was so much going on around me, so much going on in the world, so much my brain would take in and process. Expression was like a release on a pressure valve, and if I didn't release it, my mind would have probably exploded from all the things coming in. Through my writing and art, I was able to take the imaginative, evolving thoughts in my head and give them a home.

I drew pictures every day. Not just the run-of-the-mill stick figures that adorned every fridge in America, I would spend hours drawing all kinds of things. Animals, people, still lifes, vehicles, if it existed, I drew it. I loved the details and shading of the figures. I wanted them to look real. I experimented with perspective and light. One Christmas, my parents bought me a drafting table and that was it... I sat at the table for hours using all kinds of tools to perfect my craft. Comic books became great source material as I studied how the artists drew their lines, or colored and shaded their characters. It was art and through studying it, I developed an acute sense of completion and detail in all I set out to do. And it was God's blueprint for so much more.

Growing up where I did in New Jersey was like being able to see, hear, and touch every culture in one place. On my street, Italians lived next to me, Koreans across the street, a Latino family lived further down, and Jewish families lived everywhere. Welcome to the melting pot of central New Jersey, where you could go to any strip mall and shopping center and find Italians making your pizza and Asians making your Asian food. African stores owned by Nigerians that sold authentic African fashions were never hard to find. Latinos from every known Spanish-speaking country could be found in every neighborhood. Through my environment, I learned to appreciate and love all aspects of different cultures. I created an admiration and tolerance for customs I didn't fully understand. I went to dozens of ethnically diverse events from quinceañeras, to bar mitzvahs, to rights-of-passage ceremonies. Through it all, I developed an appreciation and knowledge for all kinds of people and the beauty of diversity. It also opened the door for what would be one of the most prevalent traits that trouble me to this day – having a big heart.

Being an emotionally sensitive kid was never easy. I'm not just talking about my own emotions, I loved caring for others. Empathy ruled my judgments and dealings with others. Being kind, courteous, endearing, and generous were all things I thought everyone deserved. I hated hatred – so much so, that I didn't understand it. Why bring people down when we could treat each other with respect and elevate each other's feelings? I never understood why people would treat each other so coldly and sarcastically when encouraging was so much easier for me. I never knew it then, but I lived a very sheltered existence. I also didn't know that being nice was something to be treasured; something the Holy Spirit kept within me – it was Jesus in me, screaming to be freed.

I learned quickly to hide my good nature because every day was a reminder of how the world viewed how we should treat each other. Being a Black man with a big heart didn't fit the usual stereotype. We were supposed to be hard, unconcerned, and from the hood. Our music, movies, and style said so. We couldn't be sensitive unless we wanted to be called soft or a punk. We had to lead with machismo or stay quiet in shame. These stereotypes never fit me, so I often resolved to keep to myself for fear of ostracism and inevitable insecurity. Kids on the bus would jone and taunt each other relentlessly saying countless mean things. I never knew how to join in the conversations because the venomous talk wasn't my forte. I know that it was just playful banter most of the time, but it was hard for me to tell the difference. When people would jone on me, I seldom had a quippy retort – living proof that a sharp intellect didn't always equal a sharp wit.

I could never keep up with the latest trends. Materialism was the main objective; the newest shoes and clothes were the staple of any existence back then. Despite this, girls were always giving me attention, but I could never pick up on it – naivete was the operative word here, folks. I had a big brain but never a quick wit, so I was often the butt of jokes because I couldn't keep up with the conventional mode of acceptable negativity. I would never catch on, and many of my attempts to take off my rose-colored lenses fell flat. After a while, people stopped trying to include me in the joking and "being down." Labeling me a square, a pushover, a nerd, or lame just became much easier for most. This never agreed with me.

It hurt... needing to show positivity and concern for others in a world that advertised goodwill as virtuous but deemed it weak was confusing and spiritually destructive. I would come home defeated because I couldn't understand why people were so mean. How could people use each other the way they did with such an easy conscience?

Plus, I went to private schools for most of my childhood. I was one of a few Black children in my class, very few. I had a lot of friends, or so I thought. I would get invited to all the parties and stuff. I thought many of my friends genuinely cared about me as I did for them. Looking back, I realize that many of the friends I had from school never really hung around me unless it was something school or sport related.

I'll never forget this one time I came home after a day at the little league field. The field was the local hangout spot where all the kids in town got together to eat food and candy, socialize, and watch all their friends play baseball or softball. Everyone went there. I rode my bike there regularly, alone, or with my crew when we didn't have a game in the afternoons.

One particular afternoon, I went there and rode over to my friends from the private school and received a rude awakening. I rode to one side of the bleachers and saw all the white friends from my grade and greeted them cordially as usual, but I got a less than cordial response. I sat next to my friends (or so I thought), whom I won't name, but when I got comfortable, they said,

"Hey, Jamal! Why are you over here?"

"What do you mean?"

"We know you want to sit over there with all your Black friends."

They said it as cold as that... I was like: *You are my friends. We've been in the same grade together for the past seven years. We even played on the same basketball and baseball teams at one time or another. I don't even know those kids over there like that.*

I looked at them in disbelief for a little while before I excused myself, pretending to go to the clubhouse to get some food. I went over to the "black side" of the bleachers and ran into many of the kids I either played ball with or hung out with from time to time. I didn't go to school with these public school kids, but they knew me and I knew them from the neighborhood, sports teams I played on pick-up games in the park, after-school care, and summer recreation programs.

"Hey, everyone."

A couple of snickers ensued. I spoke very properly back then. They would tell you I spoke "white." Every word and pronunciation I spoke was grounds for scrutiny. I put my bike down and sat near them on the bleachers, but not near anyone because I knew some of them a little, but not enough to feel completely comfortable as if I had seen them every day in school.

"What you doin' over here?" one of the random kids asked me.

"Watching the game and eating some food," I replied plainly.

"Why you frontin'? You know you want to be over there with your white friends."

I was stuck. The words bounced off me at first, but as I sat there feeling lonely as ever, I realized how awkward I felt – how out of place. Here I was just trying to hang out and fit in because I never said a harsh word or intentionally did a mean thing to anyone, yet for some reason, these kids wanted to make me feel less than – an outsider on all ends... It hurt. Why did everyone treat me like this when all I wanted to do was be friends and love on people?

After the games, I went home, fell face-first on my bed, and soaked my pillow. This happened often and was the backdrop for many of my experiences growing up. It hurt and was very confusing. It felt like I was always torn between two worlds, and I had a home in neither. Where did I belong?

I felt this way for a long time. These were the times when my mother would come in, sit next to me on my bed, and begin to console me. She would put her hand on my back and say stuff like, "It's okay," or "they don't deserve you." She would then sit me up and give me the biggest hugs in the world and I would empty all the tears a young boy could when his heart couldn't take feeling misunderstood anymore. Some of the frustration would go away, so I could face the rest of my day. I loved her for that. I still love her for that. In her arms, I felt like I belonged.

It was around this time in my life that my dad introduced me to a man called W.E.B. DuBois and his concept of "The Marginal Man" philosophy. To cope in this world, Black men must be able to cross the margins of society freely. They have to be able to deal with the streets and all their people as their equals in love and respect, but simultaneously be able to put on that suit and tie, uniform, or whatever and get "proper" to elevate as well. You can't just be one-dimensional. Get educated and speak properly when needed but be able to speak that slang and survive in the hood when the time comes. Navigate the streets with swagger but navigate the boardroom with intelligent and humble confidence. Learn to thrive on both sides. It's one of the mindsets I carry to this day, it's why I'm able to deal with all races, creeds, and colors in my business life, and it's one of the best pieces of wisdom my father ever gave me.

I always had the hardest time making friends. I wanted friends, but when it came time to introduce myself or be in social gatherings where I could meet new people, I would freeze. Anxiety would take over my mind and heart. It would then control my actions and my mouth so much that I appeared inept. It was hard to carry this because I knew I was smart enough to hang, but my fear of rejection made me keep my distance.

High school changed nothing. I excelled in my academics again, but my social life didn't change much. In hindsight, what strikes me is that I had no one to blame. Because I withdrew myself from many social situations, I remained a social pariah, yet in grades, extracurricular activities, and organizations, I shined. I starred in school plays, became president of my school chorus, became president of my church choir (much to the dismay of a few of our older members), representing myself and the school at many competitions, became an MC for some school functions, and became a student ambassador for various causes.

Though it looked like I had it all together on the outside, I was a conflicted soul. By the end of senior year, I had the girlfriend I always wanted, I was in the local papers for various accomplishments, and I was on my way to Morehouse College on a scholarship. None of it mattered to me. All I cared about was being happy with who I was although I had no clue who that was. It was like I was going through the motions of an overachiever (as it appeared to the adults in my town), yet my insecurities from all the years of being teased and overlooked by my peers held my mind captive – and none of the public accolades meant anything. I was still a naïve, unassuming, soft-hearted, underdog. I still had yet to see that God put another quality in me – the quality of a fighter.

I began Morehouse in the summer of '95, and boy was it a culture shock. Being a northerner in the south meant a lot of adjustment. Having to see firsthand how far slavery reached into the psyche of Black people and permanently jolted our pride and dignity, was an awakening. It also made me understand how the spirit and mentality of our people can be shifted to accept a lower position in the status quo simply by accepting the idea that we have been made less than. I thought back to Jersey and how this mindset manifested itself even in my neighborhood. The reach of systematic racism was everywhere, and I was now in the region of America that historically depended on it.

I had gone from being a minority in grade school to a multicultural high school, to a historically black college (HBCU). This is where I got to see the true beauty of my blackness – along with all its ratchetness. I loved Morehouse for its excellence and grooming in leadership, history, and intellectualism. Not only did it surround us with this academia, but it also showed us how to apply it. It allowed me to meet and grow with many brothers I'm still in touch with to this day. Yet socially, I still suffered. Don't get me wrong. I loved the friends I met, but I was still dealing with the anxieties of my past.

I went to parties, participated in auctions and shows, and I even became the president of my freshman dorm. It looked like I was about to continue to succeed as I did in high school, but I was introduced to something I never saw coming – marijuana.

Once I made her acquaintance, everything changed. I fell in love and went overboard. The wake and bake, the after class, before lunch blunt, the mid-afternoon blunt, the before dinner blunt, and the bedtime blunt. Every time I looked down at my watch (if I had one), it was 4:20. This love of getting high with my buddies did make for some special times, but it had a horrible effect that I hold responsible for the lowest parts of my college experience. It increased my already high anxiety, my low self-esteem billowed, and my innate God-given drive to perform and succeed in the classroom dwindled. Academics, the one thing I naturally overachieved in, became secondary to the desire of the stinky-sticky green.

I skipped classes. My motivation to stick to schedules took a back seat to weed. I focused on where I was going to get the next sack so I could foster my friendships with the newfound friends I made. Belonging was important to me because all my life I felt unaccepted for who I was. I partied so much and shirked so many responsibilities that by the end of my freshman year, when May arrived, the unimaginable happened. I lost my full scholarship. What made it hurt even more was that I was only required to keep a 3.0 GPA to keep my money. I got a 2.98. I was shattered. My life was ruined, and my irresponsibility made it so. What was I going to do?

Back in Jersey, there was a gentleman by the name of Malcolm Bernard. He owned a nonprofit, a foundation under his name, that would partner with corporations that would match funds to send many of the young African Americans in my town to prominent HBCUs around the country. I didn't know it, but he caught wind of my misfortune and provided my parents with a solution. He watched me come up as a young, accomplished academic in Jersey and decided to help fund the rest of my education. It was one of the first big lessons I learned in life: do the best you can all the time... You never know who's watching you.

I came back to Morehouse the next year with a vengeance. Yeah, I still smoked, but I changed my focus. I created a schedule to attend earlier classes and then go to the campus library right after classes every day. I would study for an hour or two and be done with my academics for the day by 2:00 p.m. This would leave the rest of my day for "recreation" and all the "fellowship" I wanted. By the end of my first semester of sophomore year, I ended up on the Dean's List. Not only did I learn a valuable lesson about how important it was to schedule my life for productivity, not just play, but the situation set the stage for one of the most fundamental spiritual lessons I carry to this day. If you misuse what God gives you, he may just take it away. Though I had faith in my academic ability, faith without works is dead. I'm so glad that God's grace was good enough to position Mr. Bernard in my life. He's already passed away, but second to God and my parents, I dedicate my love for the community, my life after college, and my drive in the world of education to Mr. Bernard.

Though my struggles with party substances continued throughout college (it took me six years to graduate), I made it across that stage in the spring of 2001. I regret nothing. I had met my wife three years earlier, had my own place, a job, and a car. A year later, we had our first son. We got our own place, bought a fax machine, sent out our resumes, and we ended up getting our first real jobs, together. I became a middle-school English teacher, and she became assistant to the senior vice president of a thriving yellow pages company. I loved our growing little family, and the future was bright. Everything started to work... but as you know, life has its way of switching up the game.

Materialism was never my thing. Now, I focus more on perfecting what I've already been given, not just what I want to acquire. If I keep focusing on what I want or paying attention to what I don't have, I'll keep missing out on the awesomeness and beauty of what is already in front of me, around me. I must be aware of my present to appreciate it, find pleasure in it, and see God and his wisdom in it. Otherwise, I'll keep looking past it; I'll miss seeing the blessings he's already given me.

God and I have a special relationship. Not that I want to call it special to make it that way – everyone's relationship with God is special – but when I talk about God, it just seems different from most. God and I have conversations, not just praying and talking to a seemingly empty room. We have full-blown back and forth dialogue even to the point of arguments (ones I always lose, lol). We have this dynamic: he is a father that allows me to clearly and honestly express myself with no filter. Really, what's the point of a filter when the one listening already knows what's on your mind and in your heart? I love it because it's one of the few times in my day when I feel mentally free, free from the constraints and stresses of the world, free from the judgments of others, free from the blowback of those who disagree and the impatient. He listens and he offers great advice. He never blows me off or assumes he knows what I'm going to say. He cares about what's on my mind.

For a long time, I used to wonder if that responding voice in my mind was just me, or was it truly God? Have I just been talking to myself all these years? The answer: an emphatic NO!

The Holy Spirit's always been there. I just let the world convince me to ignore him for too long. He was always the one telling me what to do whether I listened to him or not. One day, I was praying and spouting all these issues to him and I asked him an earnest question about my future, but instead of flowing into the next thought, I decided to just shut up and let him answer the question.

I was at a crossroads. I had just lost my job at the school. I had been working at a friend's start-up for months to try and generate some income, but it never panned out. My wife, my two little ones, and I just moved into our first home and had been there for a month or two by then. I was scared because I thought things would have been more stable by that point. My wife was about to lose her great paying job through it being dissolved from the economy in 2008. Bottom line: how was I going to keep food on the table? How was I going to pay the bills? How was I going to provide for my family? I asked all these questions to God on my knees, desperate for a solution. I sincerely wanted an answer from God because I had no other options at this point (which is never entirely true as it turns out).

After about a minute or two, I heard a voice in my head.

Take some of your last bit of money, get a sign saying that you will tutor, and put it on a corner in your neighborhood.

This wasn't the first time this idea had come to me. I knew there was a better way to help students learn than the traditional classroom method. I had been moonlighting as an in-home independent tutor for years while classroom teaching to help prevent students who were struggling from slipping through the cracks. He had been telling me to turn it into a tutoring business for years, but either I didn't have enough time or didn't have enough faith to believe it would work. Even when I was let go from my first teaching job, the summer before I started my second one, God asked me to step out on faith and just start my business. I didn't listen, I applied that July and found myself hired to a second school as a high school English teacher by August. I was scared, and I wanted the security of a steady income, especially since I was planning to move into a new home.

Well, the gig only lasted a year. We had moved into my mother-in-law's house to save money and transition into our new home. After that school year, I would be unemployed again, my wife would be unemployed, and I would not be able to return to the classroom due to a technicality with my certification. The idea of the business still lingered, but it was still too risky for me. I had a friend who ran a business who asked me to help him run it but found out after some time that he didn't want a partner as much as an employee. When I told him about my business idea, he entertained it at first, then said, "People aren't going to pay to be taught when they can get it for free." I almost believed him. That was 11 years ago.

My privately owned company has served over 1,100 students in my area with consistent business, mostly referral driven. I have a team of teachers that are dedicated to helping with the need for one-on-one supplemental education. I have monthly classes to prep students for the SAT, ACT, & ASVAB standardized tests. I love our students and they love us back. Not only do we tutor K-12 and college students, we mentor, encourage, and enhance them and their families. I have been to more graduation ceremonies, weddings, and family celebrations than I remember.

I have made life-long friends and mentees. The testimonies we receive are ones of love, triumph, and confidence as students and parents regularly reach their academic and life goals. Many of my high school clients have gone to college, graduated, got married, had children, etc., and I have been present at many of those special events. Moments have been shared, tears have fallen from times of duress, and relationships have been formed that I would never have had if I was still stuck in the classroom.

Currently, I am on the board of my church's private school and served as the assistant principal for this past year, until quarantine hit, and now I'm the interim principal. My business has seamlessly made the transition to independent online tutoring and test prep classes, and it's still growing. The future is bright. This tide of achievement has all been made possible because I stopped and listened to what God wanted to do with me, even when I didn't have the faith to do it myself. Eleven years ago, I put a sign on the corner when I was desperate, and now I own and operate one of the most reputable and successful tutoring companies in my county, all because I listened to God... Glory to God!!

God is in all the quiet moments – those times in the morning when I'm not trying to wake up early, but I can't get back to sleep – all alone with my thoughts. Clarity sets in among all the worries and agendas. I begin to realize how much time I waste, how much needless energy I put into unproductive things, how much I could have accomplished by now if I were to just focus my attention, or take an action that God has told me to do. Then, I make all these proclamations to God about how I'm going to do things differently and stop worrying about all the haters and logistics and just do whatever it is that has been nagging me. I do all this thinking and proclaiming to God and myself... only to finally go back to sleep and wake up later, starting my day with the same routine, to forget about the thoughts and end my day still stuck in the same stale position I was in yesterday.

I've been given all these capabilities, these talents, these gifts, and I just squander them. Or I waste them on pointed social media posts for meager approvals and temporary likes until the moment fades away into digital history – but I'm still longing for something greater. I remain unsatisfied. People don't care about my gripes and issues. They don't have a deep concern for my visions, and all the shallow accolades only amount to the equivalence of patting a dog on the head and telling him, "Good boy."

I'm tired of the mental treadmill, the monotony of the mediocre thumbs up, or the occasional heart when I know what I want is something more – the satisfaction of making a real difference in the world. The changing of someone's life, traveling to different countries, showing love to others the way Jesus did, unhindered, sharing, and trading God's wisdom with various people, giving hope to so many who seem to feel that life is just one endless cycle of impossibility after impossibility. I want others to know that they were designed to do more than their imposed limits whether the limits were self-imposed or by their environment. I know God had a reason and a purpose for giving me a gift of communication, and everything I've been through to this point has been preparing me for just the right moment to use this gift to help others see the potential that has been bestowed upon them the way God has blessed me.

This is no arrogant kick or some pang of self-importance that I have to satisfy. I simply have a strong desire to encourage others to see how special God made them. If they could see the innate talents they possess and use the God-given gifts they were blessed with, they would be able to free themselves from the depression and anxieties that hold them captive. God has enabled them with all they need; the world has convinced them that what they were given is insufficient. As a believer, I just want them to chase God, so they realize they've been living with blinders on.

I probably don't need to tell anyone this but being good is hard. In this world, although it is shown to be admirable, many times there's just not a lot of recognition for being a good, humble man. It just feels like it would be so much easier to do whatever I wanted, say whatever I wanted to anyone, or not care. Do you know how many days I just wanted to throw out all my inhibitions and forsake formalities? Cuss someone out, or give anyone a piece of my mind just to release the pressures I put up with daily? Yet, I often hold my tongue for the greater good of showing benevolence. I swallow my pride so much that people think it's an act because it can't be real. They often look right past me or think I have no backbone, so they try to take advantage of me or dismiss me.

Stuff like this has been happening to me all my life – even because of those closest to me. If I try and speak up about how my feelings get trampled on often, it's like it just gets glossed over. No one believes the happy, good guy gets spells of depression or can lose his composure. If I say anything, it gets turned into me just being self-absorbed again.

No, it's not me being self-absorbed. It's me finally saying something about it and getting tuned out. It's like people only want to deal with me when I'm in the same mood as them, otherwise, they ignore me. That's not fair. I have to deal with all of their ups and downs daily. I do my best to deal with them, but if I throw them the occasional curveball, they look the other way.

I'm tired of swallowing my pride. Matter of fact, I feel like I'm going to throw up, I've swallowed so much. I'm sick of keeping my cool when I'm constantly dealing with people who can be so combative. It feels like they are overcompensating or just plain don't know how to put their guard down around me when I'm not even on the attack. My nerves are shot because I keep getting involved in fights I never realize I'm in until the first strike is thrown. Either that or their guards are just up all the time. It's exhausting – having to work with people and their insecurities – especially ones they'll never admit to.

Though I may be tired of the conflicts, once the dust in my mind has a chance to settle, I see my inner conflicts for what they truly are. I realize that the insecurities and social awkwardness of my youth were just a training ground for keeping my composure amid adversity and misunderstandings. These things fostered my patience with people. They are the cross Jesus told me I've been assigned to carry. I've come to understand that no person who considers themselves good comes without one. I've come to welcome the challenges I have with people because God has been preparing me for them my whole life. Maturity and experience have shown me that I needed the conflicts to discover my purpose: to help and encourage others to use the God-given talents they were blessed with. All the denials and accolades, all the joys and pains, all the confidences and doubts gave me the fodder to realize I never wanted anyone to feel the way I felt. Learning to accept people the way they are with all their iniquities and imperfections – the way I wanted that acceptance growing up – has made all the difference in how I mentor and counsel others through their own perceived shortcomings into an acceptance of themselves the way God made them.

I thank God for my experiences because they fine-tuned my empathy. They enabled me to see a bit of myself in all the students and parents I try to help. I can see their inner underdog. Just because I am still a work in progress doesn't mean I can't use my gifts to help others overcome their issues. The pain and isolation I felt gave me a different type of education. While school gave me academic intelligence, life and people gave me emotional intelligence. With everything that went on in my life, sometimes it was hard to see Jesus in me crying out to be heard. With time, increasing faith, and a little spiritual maturity, I was able to find it. The connection to God's forgiving love and patience is the greatest gift I could have ever received, and I will spend the rest of my life doing the best I can to share it with others. Now, if I can just find a way to get others to spread it too. Maybe I'll get the chance to get the word out eventually on a broader level. Until then, all I can say is that my story isn't finished, and His work in me is to be continued... My internal fight is just a long-standing lesson – one that I intend to emerge as a victor. As long as others can be helped and fought for, and God is the center of my life, I will continue to be, and still be, forever a champion.

ABOUT
JAMAL L. BURT

Jamal Laurence Burt, M.Ed., is a dedicated speaker and educator that thrives on seeing people excel and achieve greatness. Mr. Burt was born into a family of educators. His mother, a teacher of 29+ years, and his sister, a teacher of 10+ years, and his father, a long-time coach and mentor to the youth in his community. always share their insights and professionalism about the craft of teaching.

He graduated in 2001 with a B.A. in English from Morehouse College and a master's degree in Educational Administration and Supervision. He has taught at the middle school, high school, and collegiate levels for over two decades, and he has founded programs for schools in the Atlanta area. He is currently the founder and owner of EBO Educational Services, LLC, a national tutoring and test prep company based in McDonough, Georgia.

His knack for connecting with his students and parents is phenomenal, and he uses these connections to create lasting bonds that have helped many of his students through high school and on into college. With a healthy dose of humor, structure, innovation, and the ability to relate to youth and adults on their level while maintaining authority, Mr. Burt has broken through to many of his students in the past and challenged them beyond their boundaries to success. The result: students at high skill levels stay challenged and students at low skill levels improve. Mr. Burt prides himself on the lasting relationships he has formed from being an educator over the years, and he continues to reach out to improve the state of learning, education, and socialization in the community.

For booking, professional tutoring, test prep services, or educational consultation, contact him at www.jamallburt.com or call 404-777-3955.

"DON'T CALL ME SIN"

by AC Scott

LOVE ME, OR LEAVE ME ALONE

I remember at 14 years of age, just starting high school, and my father came by on a Thursday evening to visit us and to give my mother some money to take care of our growing needs. My father stated that he wanted to tell me about the facts of life. I was very interested in hearing him tell me about sex, as this way I would know for sure if what I heard from friends on the street was true or not. My father walked into the kitchen to get the okay to tell me about sex while I eagerly waited in the living room. I heard him ask her if it was okay, and her response, being a Holy Ghost-filled, fire-baptized, tongue-speaking, shouting, this woman of God responded with, "...he doesn't need to know about no facts of life, he needs to be studying school." So, as he exited the kitchen and walked into the living room where I was, I knew I would have to continue learning from the streets and those who ran them. My eyes and ears were like sponges soaking up knowledge while my heart was seeking adventure. I was like a young lion walking in the Serengeti, and The High School of Art & Design was my watering hole. I was exposed to various types of young women, from Asian, West Indian, Latin (Puerto Rican & Dominican), Caucasian, and African American. The beauty of this was they were from all over the five boroughs; there were so many women to choose from... It was as if I was at a buffet. I was going to enjoy exiting my shell.

Over the next few months, I was getting information from all sources, such as guys from school, gang members, various family members, as well as friends in the neighborhood. Then one day while ditching school, one of the guys from my hood suggested going to the Ascot to see a movie. My response was, "What's the Ascot?" A couple of them laughed and said, "It's a porno movie theatre." It sounded interesting so we all agreed and went. As we approached the movie theatre, everybody put their hoodies over their heads; after all, it was the middle of the day and we didn't want to be recognized since we did live in the Bronx so there was no telling who might be walking by. We entered the theatre and began to spread out, not close to anyone, but close enough so that if any of us had any beef with a rival posse, we would be near to give them "the Bronx beat down."

As I watched the movie, I was amazed at what I saw. It's one thing to discuss it and hear about it, and it's another to visualize it and then some. I couldn't wait to try some of the things I viewed, as I contemplated which girl I would use them on first.

God is an awesome God, especially in our foolish state. He prepares us for things when we're not prepared. My mother took me to the doctor so I could get a physical done for school. After the physical, the nurse asked my mother to step out of the room for a moment. The nurse then asked me if I was having sex yet. I reluctantly answered yes. She asked if I was using protection. I thought, what's protection, I didn't hear anything about protection when talking about sex with my street consultants and friends. And I sure didn't see anything about protection when I saw the movie. It probably showed all over my face that I didn't have a clue about protection. She said, "I'll be right back," as she disappeared from the examination room. I waited with anticipation for her to return, still pondering about "protection." To my surprise, the nurse handed me a brown paper bag, tightly wrapped, while she explained that inside the bag were condoms. I was shocked, thinking my mother was right on the other side of the door. I knew she would not be pleased. Remember how she reacted when my father wanted to have "that talk"? This is where professional sex education began. The nurse informed me on how to use them and when to use them. I can't recall what was going through my mind, because I was shocked by the words that were coming out of her mouth. She proceeded to tell me that every time I had sex, I should wear one, to prevent sexually transmitted diseases as well as to prevent pregnancies. The nurse made it a point to tell me not to believe when a woman says she's on the pill and to always use a condom. That resonated as I left the office with a lingering smile. That day, I was given a license to have sex when I exited the doctor's office with a bag full of condoms in my pocket. It was on like hot buttered popcorn! With condoms and the moves, and information from the movie at the Ascot, I was ready to go out on the prowl and slay some punani.

As I began exploring with various young women, there was one who caught my attention. She was two years older than me. I always had a strong attraction for the older woman. I scheduled to meet her at her place. After dinner, we sat in the living room and watched television while her mother went to answer the phone in the bedroom. The young lady informed me that her mother would be on the phone for hours since she was talking to her sister. I remember placing my hands on her legs and I said to her, "Let's F***. She looked at me as if I had lost my mind and replied, "You don't know a better way to say that?" I was at a loss for words. After all, that's the way the men said it in the movie; hell, the women said the same thing. I sat there for at least 45 minutes, contemplating whether I should grab my coat and leave or figure out a nicer way of saying it. So, I looked at her and asked, "Can I make love to you?" and she smiled and said, "Was that so hard?"

A new adventure began as we were about to have sex while her mother was in the next room. That was such an exciting rush! She was impressed with what I knew and was capable of since I was younger than her. Over the next few months, she showed me how impressed and appreciative she was. And I was developing feelings for her. When I wasn't hanging with the fellas, we were enjoying each other's company, when her mother was home and when she wasn't home. I thought I was in love until she broke my heart. She got involved with an older cat and decided to start a life with the dude.

So, after going through the situation, I started listening to the streets again. I decided that love wasn't for me. Over the next few years, my motto was, "Amuse me, or lose me." I was never that brother who wanted to hit it the first night – you had to tease me, and I didn't want it if it was that easy. At the same time, this wasn't going to be a calculus problem where it would take months to grasp the concept. My thing was that if I didn't hit it within two weeks, a month tops, depending on the female, I was out. This brother wasn't interested anymore. I was Audi 5000, gone with the wind. If I did hit, I stayed around as long as she could keep my interest. Even during those times, I looked for quality, not quantity. I still had to have some sort of engaging conversations to see where her head was at; I didn't want to connect with stalkers or drama queens. I didn't realize it at the time, but this brother became arrogant. You couldn't tell me that it wasn't about me and if you tried, I attributed it to the other person being jealous of who I was or who I thought I was.

By 17, I changed up my appearance. When hanging with the fellas, it was Timberland boots unless we were going on the prowl or out to the clubs, and then it was my apparel of choice ...slacks or jeans, dress shoes, or British Walkers, or even Clarks. They came in various colors so a brother could stay coordinated with the shirts or leather sweaters picked up from Delancey Street. There were two reasons for the change in how I dressed. Firstly, at that time there was a lot of racial profiling by the police, so if they stopped a young Black or Hispanic man hoping to get lucky and get him for a crime, their response when stopping him was, "We just got a call and you fit the description." After all, this was the hip hop era, so most people dressed to fit the culture. I tried to stay fresh by switching up the style so if I was stopped by the police, they would have to have more than, "You fit the description." Really, what was the description of the alleged perpetrator? Secondly, I was tired of talking to women my age. I wanted the adventure and challenge of older women, so to do that I needed to switch gears. I didn't realize I was linking my identity to that of a woman's man or player, and that it didn't fit with who God said I was.

ME, MYSELF, AND I

The Eighties was a special era. Hip hop was exploding with rap, breakdancing, and graffiti. I was coming of age to enjoy the whole culture. I used to practice writing rhymes and rap as well as tagging (the art of writing a nickname or mark to a surface - book, wall, bus, train, and/or bridge by a graffiti artist). Growing up, I was quiet and a bit shy. I remember two of my older female cousins talking about me one day. The older one stated, ".... wait 'till he breaks out of his shell, he's going to be something else." She was right.

I would watch shows such as Saturday morning martial arts movies, the Adventures of Hercules, Ali Baba and the Forty Thieves, and the Seven Voyages of Sinbad. During this time, people were picking out nicknames that described who they were such as Grandmaster Flash, Slick Rick, KRS-One, LL Cool J, Big Daddy Kane, Kid & Play. I selected "Sinbad." After all, I was searching for adventure and this was the beginning of my voyage to discover who I am.

Growing up in a Pentecostal church, I was in church every time the doors opened: Sunday morning – all day, starting at 9:00 a.m. for Sunday School and an 11:30 a.m. church service that didn't end until 3:00 p.m. After service, we had lunch at the nearby McDonald's or Chinese restaurant, and then go back to church for another service starting at 5:00 p.m. which ended at about 8:30 p.m. Then the parents would talk and engage in fellowship for another 30 or 40 minutes, which kept us at church after dark. Then there was Tuesday night prayer at 7:00 p.m. and Saturday morning choir rehearsal starting at 9:00 a.m., finishing around noon. Then it would start all over again on

Sunday. If there was a church anniversary or special service, it was worse as we wouldn't leave church 'till around 11:00 p.m.

As a teenager entering high school, I was trying to discover how to be a man, and what kind of man I was supposed to be. My parents were separated so my brother and I didn't have a male role model living in our household, and though we had uncles, it wasn't the same. They weren't easily accessible when we had questions about life, so the streets started calling. Traveling back and forth to go to school from the Bronx to Manhattan began to give me a sense of independence. I was 14 years old, taking the subway into the city alone, and that was an amazing experience. The very first time I was nervous, but after a week it was a great teacher. It taught me to be aware of my surroundings and how to detect danger. I started meeting and interacting with people from all areas of the five boroughs and of various ethnicities. It was exciting, and my shell was beginning to crack.

During my first year of high school, I was asked to join the Five-Percent Nation of Gods and Earths, an offshoot of the Nation of Islam. I was informed that the Nation would help give me knowledge of self. This appeared to be exactly what I was looking for, as well as a new adventure. My nickname "Sinbad" was put to the side and I was given the name "Supreme Justice God Allah." I was also given a packet consisting of my daily mathematics to study and know verbatim, when meeting up with other gods or earths, and to be prepared for any ciphers (a 360-degree circle which we would be in, and then expand on the lessons of the day including mathematics). If a person didn't know or remember the lesson for the day, they had a choice of punishment – either mental justice where none of the gods or earths would speak to you for the entire day or physical justice where the person was subjected to being pummeled by fists for a specific amount of time.

I stayed in this organization for about six months, and although it gave me an awareness of Black history, it also gave the appearance of hate against white people or as the nation called them, "Devils." During this time, I had a few associates who were members of the Almighty Zulu Nation who asked me to attend a rally that they were having in Soundview Projects in the Bronx. After the rally, I was asked if I'd be interested in joining. I needed time to think as I didn't want to rush into anything. After two weeks, I decided to join and the name "Sinbad" was back in play. The enemy has a way of using people and things. At times people would call me "Sin" for short and during the next two years, I was walking in Sin.

Still trying to find my identity, I was associating the name to who I was, even wearing a belt buckle with the word Sin boldly displayed on it for the whole world to see, and brazen enough to wear it to church on several occasions until one Sunday when a woman who was like a second mother to me, pulled me to the side and talked to me. She didn't yell at me, she didn't talk to me, but she spoke to me and asked me not to wear it at church. She stated that she understood that it was my nickname in the streets, but it wasn't appropriate for the house of the Lord or how it made my mother look. It warmed my heart that she took the time to explain the appearance of my actions. I smiled and agreed to tone it down when I came to church. I stopped wearing the Sin belt buckle and replaced it with skull and crossbones.

I was learning so much from the streets, my fellow students, and the gang. I associated with car thieves, drug dealers, gang members, felons, and a few killers. I was a student at the School of Hard Knox, and I was placing my identity with the things I was doing or associated with. But God...the Lord knew that I might have done some of the things that were stated but he also knew that's not who I was.

My last year of high school was the turning point for me. One of the older members of the Zulu Nation pulled me to the side to talk to me. It appeared that he was leaving the organization and going into the military, and the recruiter had told him to get as many young men out of the gang before we made a mess out of our lives. I happened to be one of those individuals. His words were, "Hey, Young Blood, this life ain't for you." I questioned him as to how he came to that conclusion. He chuckled and said, "No disrespect Sin, but I've been watching you and there's something different about you. You're one of the first ones to respond when others have beef, but when you have beef you don't ask for help, you handle it on your own." He was right but I didn't think anyone noticed, and I sure didn't think it was because I was special. You learn a lot in these streets and one thing I learned is that I had trust issues. I've seen people turn on each other when facing time. My thought process was that if they didn't know what you do, they can't tell on you. My motto was like Treach from naughty by nature, "I do my dirt all by my lonely." So, I went home and thought about what he said and by the end of the week, I decided that he might be right and I should continue being my own person and look for new adventures...just me, myself, and I.

THE BARREL OF THE GUN

As I looked down the barrel of the black steel, I was stunned that this was happening to me. Sin was being robbed? Two Hispanics were robbing me of my jewelry. The first one had the gun aimed at my face, while the second one snatched the chains off my neck and then proceeded to remove the rings from my fingers. I heard the one with the gun say, "Don't move and I won't shoot." Many thoughts were rushing through my mind. Should I rush the one with the gun? Should I grab the second one and use him as a shield? Should I push the alarm of the elevator and hope the guys in front of the building would come running in to see what was going on? There I was, of all nights, without my gun. The second guy stepped back, while the first guy held his gun aimed directly at me as he backed out from blocking the elevator doors from closing. They took off running as the elevator door closed. As the elevator began to ascend, I swiftly pressed the third-floor button as it passed the second floor. The doors opened on the third floor and I raced down the barely lit staircase of the housing projects to see if I could catch them. As I arrived on the first floor, I tried to figure out if they had exited by the front of the building or the back. Adrenaline pumping, I raced to the front of the building and out the door, never once thinking that I didn't have my pistol on me. I asked one of the guys hanging out in front of the building, "Did you see two Puerto Ricans come out of the building?" Growing up in the Bronx allowed me to distinguish the Puerto Rican accent from the Dominican accent. He responded, "Nah, what's up?" I ignored his question as I headed for the train station since that's where I first spotted them while leaving the train station. I figured they must have followed me to my building.

As I reached the subway, I raced down the stairs, and it sounded like a train had arrived. I got to the tollbooth, jumped the turnstile, and proceeded to run down some more stairs to the uptown 6 train platform. The doors began to close as I yelled, "Hold the train!" but to no avail. As I reached the bottom of the platform, the train pulled out of the station and headed uptown. Angry, NO, pissed the hell off, I headed back upstairs and back to my building, not accepting that I had just been jacked. It's a feeling that leaves you with a sense of vulnerability and violation. When I entered my apartment, I headed straight to my room and closed the door behind me. I opened my drawer and pulled out my gun as the thoughts of being robbed continued to race through my mind. I started thinking and remembered seeing the two guys on the train. They were in the same car, sitting further down. When I got off, they got off. Both men went up the stairs before me and exited the train station first. They were at the corner at the phone booth. I thought they were making a phone call. I continued walking to my building, not once looking back. After all, I was on "my" block, so I got lax and let my guard down. I couldn't believe it. I have been in different areas of four of the five boroughs, Brooklyn, Queens, Manhattan, and even the Bronx, and have never been robbed and tonight it happens in my area, in my building. And on a night when I didn't have my partner with me – my gun, my .45. All because I was visiting my girl in Queens, and I wanted to respect her parents and their home by not bringing a weapon, especially an illegal weapon, into their home. I guess that's what love gets you, "...Assed out." My gold was gone, and my pride, bruised.

Looking back now love is what saved me, the love of God. I bet you thought I was going to say the love of my girl saved me. I never get it twisted. God was with me all along. Things could have turned out differently, but God loved me that much that he allowed me to come through it all unharmed.

NEW ADVENTURES

The day came when I had to leave the gang life and had to stop running around with different women. After spending time with one woman, I realized she was who I wanted to spend the rest of my life with. She had a style, unlike other women I knew. She had a business mind that was different from most women I knew. For a long time, she was able to keep me amused without having to have sex. I enjoyed her company. She was different from the others. Some satisfied me sexually but did nothing for me intellectually, while others were fun to be around but were a waste of time, sexually. There were a few who had drama, and I don't do drama. After a two-year engagement, I was on the verge of starting a new adventure from fiancé to husband. So now I was also placing my identity in being a husband and father.

It was time to let my mother know that her oldest son was moving out. As I looked into her eyes, I saw the shock mixed with pride. She was a beautiful, smart woman with class and style, and has tripled in wisdom to this day. She taught my siblings and me that just because you live in the projects you don't have to act like your environment. She was a God-fearing woman who was stern but fair.

As I stood before the woman that single-handedly raised me, I remembered the night she found out I was carrying a gun. She was sitting in the kitchen waiting for me to come home. I entered the apartment after hanging out with the fellas, and she stopped me at the door. I was a little surprised that she was not in bed sleeping. She immediately asked me what was in my jacket. "Nothing," I responded. She said, "Open your jacket." My heart was racing and I didn't know what to do or say. I was trying to figure out why was she asking me about what was in my jacket. Did someone rat me out? Did God drop it in her spirit since she had such a close connection with him?. I zipped down my jacket, partially hoping she didn't see it. I heard the anger in her voice as she told me to open my jacket all the way. The sweat was dripping from the top of my head as I opened my jacket. I now witnessed the anger and disappointment in her eyes as I opened my jacket, and low and behold, there was the nickel-plated .45 that I carried on me. 'Justin' was what I called it – just in case I was in a situation that warranted extra security that my hands might not be able to handle. After all, we did not live in the safest of neighborhoods. She asked me what I was doing with that gun. In my mind, I was thinking, Mom, are you serious? I live in the Bronx. But my mouth said that I was holding it for a friend. She scolded me for a moment and told me to turn around and take the gun back to where it came from and to never bring it in the apartment again. She also warned me, "If you ever bring that gun in here again, I'll call the police on you." As I walked to one of my homeboy's place to ask him to hold my gun until the heat wore down, I thought about my mom's reaction. New York was different than most places in the south and the Midwest. Guns were illegal unless you were law enforcement or had a special permit. I was thankful for her fairness because she could have called the police first with no warning, and this brother would have had his first strike. Thank you, Lord. I also thank God for a God-fearing mother that loved me enough to protect me from myself.

Later, there I was, on my own, a hard-working family man, husband, and father. There were challenges and rough spots in our marriage as well as good times, times when I wished I had someone to guide or mentor me, but didn't always have that. I didn't have anyone to instruct me on how to be a husband so there were some things I was doing wrong. I had good intentions but they were being carried out wrong. Because this woman, now my wife, was the best thing that had entered my life, and I cherished her, loved her, and worshipped her. It's okay to cherish someone, even to love someone. but it's a problem to worship anyone. I stopped worshipping the one who gave me the gift and began worshipping the gift. And as the word of God states, "I'll have no other God before me." Throughout the years, we had good times, bad times, uphill battles, and great victories. Raising kids, buying our first house, employed in various careers. In one of the storms of life, God had to show me that my priorities were wrong, and I needed to put things back into their correct perspective.

After all, God is a God of order and things were becoming chaotic. I got to a point where I couldn't function, emotionally or spiritually. Physically, I was just existing. Thank God for a second chance. No, thank God for another chance. God spent time with me in isolation and gave me another chance to put things in their proper order. He also showed me that my identity wasn't wrapped up in being a husband or a father. I was so much more than I realized. I am not the mistakes I've made in my past. I'm not the failures that have occurred in my life. My identity was tied to my relationship with God the father. And God said that I am loved, that I am his, I am worthy, I am purposed, and I am redeemed. Don't call me Sin!

Throughout my time of isolation, he reminded me, "I have called you by name; you are mine." God shaped me as a potter does clay. "I have called you and I have chosen you. You have a glorious future. You are an ambassador for Christ." God showed me that the enemy used the fact that I was an adventurer, and when I picked the name Sinbad, it was a trick of the enemy in that when it was used in its short form, it was a sin. I was missing the mark. That's what sin is, missing the mark. He was also making me think that God didn't love me because of the name "Sin".

God hates the sin that we perform but God loves us. He sent His only begotten son to die for our sins. The name you choose doesn't determine your adventures. My first name is Arnold which means 'bold as an eagle,' which I have displayed, time and time again in these cold streets. Christopher is my middle name and it means 'Christ-bearer', and I have carried Him with me all my life. It was the Christ I was carrying in my heart that wouldn't allow me to do certain things in those streets. It was the love of Christ that had me praying for some of my associates who were committing various crimes. It was the heart of Christ that allowed me to forgive those who betrayed me. It was the peace of Christ that kept me sane when there were times, I should have lost my mind. I thank God for giving me another chance. (A.C.) I thank God for being chosen to be an Ambassador for Christ. (A.C.) I thank God for being anointed and commissioned. (A.C.) I thank God for my assignment and my calling (A.C.) I thank God for assured confidence (A.C.) in Him.

Another thing God showed me while watching TBN one night, was actor Gary Busey being interviewed, and if you want an adventure, you can have Fantastic Adventures in Trusting Him. Wow, F.A.I.T.H. It will take you on some amazing adventures as it strengthens from faith to faith.

Growing up in the church, the elders only showed one side of God – the disciplinarian. If you don't live right, you're going to hell. If you don't talk right, you're going to hell. If you don't walk right, you're going to hell. Everything that didn't line up to the word, you're going to hell. I get it, but they never spoke of the loving side of God, that He forgives, He's a God of peace and comfort. I left the church to search and discover who I was and who I was supposed to be, only to be led back to the one who had all the answers; not the church, but GOD.

Looking back over my life, I have had some physical, emotional, and financial battles. There were some battles that I won, some that tried to knock me down, but never did I lose. Instead, I learned. I learned how to get back up and keep going. I learned how to maneuver through and around certain situations. I learned how to block certain blows. I have learned how to deliver blows, but most of all, regardless of what adventures and battles I have endured, I am still standing! I am still here! I am still a Champion!

ABOUT
AC SCOTT

AC Scott was born in the inner city in the Bronx, New York. He has worked in the healthcare field for over 25 years. He is a Life Coach and uses his spiritual gift of encouragement to help men that God places in his life. He believes in being "his brother's keeper."

AC is a chaplain and a member of the Global Chaplain Coalition (GCC). As a chaplain, he recognizes that although cultures and traditions vary from country to country, human suffering is global, and therefore has dedicated himself to living out God's Great Commission by being a missionary to the Nations. AC is a missionary to South Africa, Dominican Republic, and an ordained minister to Living Sacrifice Prophetic Ministries in Trinidad and Tobago.

AC and his wife are leaders of the "LOVING YOU UNTIL" Marriage Ministry through which they counsel married couples and those seeking to join in Holy Matrimony. Their purpose is to help save one marriage at a time. They have also launched Global Connections Academy and Global Connections Ministries International. Chaplain AC spent five years as a radio personality and co-producer of a radio show in South Florida. Chaplain AC is married to his wonderful wife of 33 years and has three children and four grandchildren! He gives God all the praise for his amazing family.

He believes that everyone has untapped greatness that God has placed within and it is imperative to find it and live the abundant life that Jesus intends for each of us.

TRANSFORMED FROM DARKNESS TO LIGHT

by Prince Blair

Better late than never. I was supposed to write this book 38 years ago. An elderly man told me, "Prince, you should write a book about your life," and of course I heard him, but did not listen. Nevertheless, I have a lot more life experience to share now. These are some of the stories that illustrate the different episodes of my life: Young Prince, Prince the Man, Prince Charming, Prince of Darkness, Prince the Chosen One, Prince of Peace, and Prince the Champion.

YOUNG PRINCE

I was raised by a single mother in Queens, New York, with two sisters, one older, Marandia, and one younger, Sandye, which I call "Over" and "Under." My mother is the strongest woman I have ever known. I watched her struggle yet persevere for her children. I think I nearly drove my mother crazy as a young boy. The reason why I say this is because I received a lot of beatings growing up, and I probably deserved all of them. I believe that my mother was trying to beat the hell out of me, but and at the same time, love the hell out of me. One thing that we did not lack in our household was love. We always had plenty to eat, clean clothes, and we had good times.

My mother raised us in the church. We attended the First Baptist Church in Queens. My mother would give me money to put into the church offering, but on the way there, my sisters and I would stop at the bakery and buy jelly donuts, which were my favorite. Mother always dressed my sisters and me in our finest church clothes to go to church. But as a boy, I didn't know any better, so I either got dirty or fell and ripped holes in the knees of my pants and of course, I got a beating for that. When we got to the church, I went straight up to the balcony to watch the live show. I couldn't wait to see who was going to be the first person to receive the Holy Ghost as for me, that was the most exciting part of the service.

In our church, Pastor Gardner, and the entire congregation were Black. I was always perplexed about the giant picture that hung high up on the wall right in the center of the church. It was a picture of Jesus Christ with blonde hair, blue eyes, and white skin. As a child, I asked my mother, "Why is Jesus white in that picture?" and she replied, "It doesn't matter what color his skin is." Being a young boy, I didn't question my mother's answer, but I still wondered why he was white with blonde hair and blue eyes if it didn't matter. When I was baptized, that picture of Jesus was right over the baptismal pool. I was more afraid of the picture than being baptized. It seemed like Jesus' blue eyes were focused only on me and every time I looked at that picture, he would not take his eyes off me. When Pastor Gardner submerged me underwater, I thought I was drowning. I was so happy when it was over that I could not stop laughing.

Ms. Eloise, that's my mother's name, loved us more than anything in the world. I watched my mother struggle and sacrifice for me and my sisters. I remember as a boy, walking my mother up the street to go to work, and watching her disappear into the darkness. She worked in a sub-standard job with long hours and low pay to put herself through nursing school, and became a registered nurse, graduating with honors. When she came home from work, she never complained about how tired she was, and she loved on her children. One day, Mother told me that her children were her reason for living. My sisters and I were always so happy when Mother came home because she always brought a surprise for us that made us happy. We would jump around and yell loudly, "Yay, Momma's home," sounding like a three-person chorus. That was the best part of my day.

My mother, as a God-fearing woman, was trying to deal with the behaviors of a boy without a father. I think it worked for a while but as I got older, things began to change. Growing up in East Elmhurst, Queens, NY, I had a lot of fun as a young boy in our neighborhood. It was a low-income neighborhood filled with mostly Black and Hispanic families. We played all the time on our block. The unwritten rule was that we never leave our block, as that was a major offense. In our neighborhood, we had many mothers, and everyone looked out for each other. We lived by the African proverb, "It takes a village to raise one child." If your mother wasn't around, the other mothers would quickly put you in check. They would tell us to get out of the street so we wouldn't get hit by a car, to stop throwing rocks, to watch our mouths, and sometimes, they would say, "Come here, boy," and bless you out, right then and there. We didn't have video games, cell phones, Instagram, TikTok, and all these social media gadgets that young people have nowadays. We played outside games like tag, hide and go seek, football in the street, red light green light 123, RCK, racing, and basketball with the garbage can as the basket. We knew that we had to be inside our house if our mother called us out the window or before the streetlights came on.

Through elementary, junior high, and high school, my grades were average. During my school days, I was teased a lot because of the way I dressed, with high-water pants, suspenders, and PF Flyers sneakers. The other kids made fun of my younger sister Sandye because of her glasses and they would tease her by saying she had Coca-Cola bottles on her eyes. Needless to say, to defend me and my sister, I got into a lot of fights. My first encounter was with Steven, the neighborhood bully. He bullied me for weeks and I was afraid to fight him because of his reputation. One day he followed me home from school and the crowd that wanted to see a fight followed him. I ran inside and my mother was already home so she asked me who all those kids were outside. She took me back outside and made me fight the bully. She coached me and clearly said that if I didn't beat him, she would beat me. I was more scared of my mother than Steven. I remember beating Steven until he gave up and I never had a problem with him again.

The next encounter I had with a bully was in junior high school; a girl named Raydell. She was a real big girl who beat up a lot of boys. One day she got in my face and I was afraid of her, but I was taught to never hit girls. So, my options were fight or flight. I chose flight. I ran as fast as I could and when I got home, I told my big sister Marandia. The next day, she came to the school and stepped up to the bully, hard, and I never had a problem with her again. The values that you are raised with will never leave you. My mother always taught me to never put my hands on a lady, and if you ever thought about it, you were having a nightmare, so slap yourself and wake up. I believe everything we go through in life will teach us something if we learn from it. That is a major principle when it comes to being a strong man, a CHAMPION.

After the lesson comes the blessing is one of my favorite sayings, and it has a deeper meaning. The working definition is that if you don't learn from your bad behavior then it is likely that you will keep repeating that behavior and the penalty will be severe. The Bible says, "The beginning of wisdom is this: Get wisdom. Though it costs all you have, get understanding." (Proverbs 4:7 NIV) Wisdom is the principal thing, therefore get wisdom, and with all of thy getting, get understanding. Understanding is the best part. It makes things clear in your mind. It's called clarity.

My mother was my very first teacher. What she did not know in wisdom, she made up for with love. One of the main reasons I love my mother so much is that she was my god. I know this because God is love. There has never been a time in my life when my Queen Mother hasn't shown me love. In my deepest heart, I truly believe that I am alive today because my mother prayed for me without ceasing. I had too many close calls with death to think otherwise.

I never saw my father in my entire life and I often wondered what type of man he was. One night, late in the evening as a young boy, I remember hearing the doorbell ring several times from our upstairs apartment, and I yelled, "Who is it?" A man said his name several times. I responded, "Who are you?"

and his deep voice replied, "I am your father." I ran to tell my mother that the man at the door said he was my father. Mother rushed to the door and told me to go back inside. She had a look of disappointment and anger on her face and somehow, I knew it was serious. From behind the door, I heard a lot of yelling back and forth. Mother slammed the door and came back inside. When she came back in, I asked her, "Was that my father?" She looked at me straight in the eye and said, "I am your father and your mother, and don't ever ask me that question again as long as you live." And I never did. For the next several decades I never really thought about my father at all. Looking back at all the mistakes I've made, I do think that if I had the guidance of a good father, I would have avoided a lot of my mistakes because only a man can show a boy how to be a man. The African proverb says, "A boy is the only thing God can make a man out of."

During my high school days, I started becoming more independent. I remember that my mother always told me that I was the man of the house. I didn't know what that meant but I wanted to live up to the task. In my last year of high school, my best friend Ron and I joined the military in a Delay Entry Program (D.E.P). As a result of our joining this program, two big pictures of Ron and I were displayed in the main office of my high school that we didn't even know about. I found out from many of the other students in the school who told me they saw my picture in the office. At first, I was very upset, but I couldn't do anything about it. The lesson learned was: always ask many questions until you are clear with all the details. The flip side to this high school episode was that my best friend and I became overnight high school stars.

My days in high school became very interesting, to say the least. I remember in my very last semester of 12th grade, I was told that I would not be graduating with my class. I was so upset about this news and I did not want to tell my mother because she would be so disappointed. I went to my guidance counselor to plead my case. Dr. Thompson was her name, and she was the head of the English department and my English teacher. As I continued to plead my case, she told me that I failed a term of English and I would need to write a four-page book report on a book by Shakespeare, in one week. I became frustrated because I didn't understand Shakespeare. I hated reading it because it was like a foreign language. I thought to myself, "How in the world am I going to do this?" It seemed to be the longest walk home as I felt sad, heartbroken, and hopeless, and as if my little world was coming apart right before my eyes. Not knowing God on a personal level but having a praying mother that always prayed without ceasing for her children, I truly believed she spent a little extra time talking to God about her wonderful son. When I got home that day, I was a little relieved because my mother wasn't home from work yet, so I told my sisters the bad news. My big sister Marandia was the smartest in the house and she knew Dr. Thompson very well. I think she was one of Dr. Thompson's favorite students since she was an English major. Marandia had already read the book that Dr. Thompson asked me to write about and she got an A in her class. Needless to say, Marandia helped me with my book report and I passed the class and was able to graduate on time with my classmates. To God be the Glory.

PRINCE THE MAN

I had a short stay in the United States Military where I learned all about weapons. I learned the technology of weapons and explosives in the best school in the world. I became a weapons specialist. I always had a fascination with the power of guns. Discharged from the military because I had a problem with authority, I received a general discharge under honorable conditions. When I went back home to the streets of New York, one of the first things I did, was purchase a gun. In New York City, a virtual innocent can obtain any type of firearm, 24 hours a day, seven days a week, if you know the right person.

(Episode 1)

The first time I committed a crime was because I wanted to take my girlfriend to the movies and didn't have any money. I had a gun, was trained, and had the heart to use it. So, I thought to myself, that I would rob someone for their money. Knowing guys that had robbed before and got a lot of money, I thought to myself, how hard could it be? I practiced doing robberies like rehearsing for a movie, but it was not a movie, it was real. I stalked my victim like a lion watching his prey and figured out a plan. I went to the local bank and watched people go in and out of the bank from the parking lot. They were carefree with their money and were not paying attention to their surroundings. Knowing the advantage that the robber has is the element of surprise while shocking his victim, I robbed an older couple at gunpoint and took over $300 in cash from them. At that moment I thought I was rich. It had given me a rush and it was easy money. I knew that whoever holds the gun has the power and it was so easy that I started robbing for the fun of it. I was a product of my environment and didn't even know it. As I graduated to bigger crimes, I joined a stick-up crew that I knew and we planned robberies in the boroughs of Queens, Brooklyn, The Bronx, and Manhattan. At this time, we were mostly robbing other drug dealers because they couldn't report the crime to the police. We became efficient, aggressive, and dangerous. Our robberies were carefully planned and executed to the detail. As fate would have it, when you keep getting and getting, you forget that you could be got. That's slang for what goes around comes around. Oh yeah, I forgot to mention that I have a Ph.D. degree in street intelligence which I will never forget, and still have street tendencies. Pray for me.

The street taught me this, save me from my friends because I know my enemies. Friends are the ones that you let get close to you and then you put your guard down and they take advantage of you. Every time something happened with the monies in the crew, it was always an inside job because there is no honor among thieves. Many people are book smart, but they have no street smart. The secret is to have both, like me. I attended ITT College and Nyack Seminary College and I'm thankful for my formal education, but the real gift is knowing when and how to use both.

As we graduated to more advanced levels of crime, we started robbing all sorts of businesses, always well-planned and executed. Many robberies were planned during bad storms because we knew that the police didn't drive around a lot, and if they were called, it would take a while for them to get to the location. At this point, I was a professional criminal, in that I functioned in the underworld. I considered myself a vampire because I only came out a night. I wasn't very much into the club scene but in the after-hours clubs, I was comfortable. The majority of people in the after-hours were hustlers, gamblers, drug dealers, wild ladies, and criminals. The talk was negative, the element was dangerous, and it was a dog-eat-dog environment; fast cash, fast cars, fast girls, fast everything. Remember, this was the City of New York, the city that never sleeps.

PRINCE CHARMING

Unlike most people, I never looked forward to the weekend. Thursdays, Fridays, and Saturdays were my hustle days and I stayed up and hustled three days straight, week after week after week. If you wonder how I did that, I was using high-quality cocaine that kept me up and alert for those 72 hours. During those three days, I only came home to shower, change my clothes and my jewelry. I always took pride in how I dressed, from top to bottom, and was always fresh from head to toe. That's what made me The Prince of New York. So much happened during those three days. My security stayed close because they knew I was the man, and I would take care of them. Because of who I was in the game, I attracted a lot of attention from females (groupies) so I was able to pick, choose, and refuse whoever I wanted. As I had established my reputation in the drug world as an alpha male, many females called me Prince Charming. In the clubs they wanted to be in my presence, living the champagne life. Sex, money, and drugs were the lifestyle.

Keep in mind that fast money spends fast. It almost seemed surreal because it was like a non-stop action movie and I played the lead role. As fate would have it, I was arrested and went to jail on a robbery charge because someone snitched. Remember, there is no honor among thieves. The police arrested me coming out of my apartment and I was convicted and sentenced to two to six years for my first offense and was sent to a prison in upstate New York. Although it was my first offense in a court of law, in my heart I knew that I had got away with many armed robberies. Going to prison for the first time was scary but I adjusted to prison life because of my military training. During my time there, I was not rehabilitated but became more criminally-minded because of the element around me. This was the making of the Prince of Darkness.

PRINCE OF DARKNESS

(Episode 2)

They tried but they missed. Shortly after coming home from prison, I got back into the drug game. My crew consisted of four seasoned street veterans but I only trusted the one who I knew the longest. I was fearless, the enforcer on the team, meaning the muscle. I was strategic, ruthless, and deadly because I was always strapped and knew the power of the gun. I remember very vividly that on this particular night, we went to make a big drug deal with our connection with whom we had done several deals, and they had always gone smoothly. They had never tried to rob us before.

As I was preparing mentally for this deal, I had a weird feeling. Normally, I didn't wear my bulletproof vest to drug deals but for some reason, that night I did. This was not a normal drug deal as we were carrying over $50,000 in cash, and the other deals were usually about $25,000. This is the part of the drug world that most people don't know about. They see the flash, bling-bling, cars, jewelry, and stacks of cash, but this was the dangerous part of the business. For this part, I transformed into another person. I didn't like anyone talking to me on the way to do the deals. The rules were: one person talked, and he was called the dealmaker, and everyone else was on point and watched his back. The place where the business transaction would occur was already agreed upon in advance, so there wouldn't be any surprises. However, this was the underworld, and surprises were expected.

For this deal, we drove in two separate cars, two in two. The first car was used as a decoy in case we ran into 5-0 on the way back. The other car was the money car. On this night, everything happened so fast, you couldn't blink your eyes. The deal went bad because it was a setup. They tried to rob us of our money and had no intention of making the deal. "Are you crazy?" I thought to myself. We were all stickup men. Gunfire rang out like in a movie scene, but it was not a movie, this was as real as it gets. My heart pounded and my adrenalin took over. They must have known who I was because most of the bullets came my way. I got shot twice that night, once in my chest and the other bullet grazed my right leg. The bullet that hit me in the chest was so strong that it knocked me off my feet, but I jumped back up and kept shooting in their direction. One of our crew members got shot badly and we had to leave him, but the rest of us got away safely. I drove home alone, and all kinds of thoughts raced through my head. I thought, "Was it a setup by someone on our team? Was I the target? Was I going to bleed to death? (There was a lot of blood on my clothes.) Was I going to live or die?" I wanted to get back to my safe place.

When I got there, my chest was burning like fire. The pain was unbearable, and it hurt more than anything that I had ever felt. I saw the amount of blood on my clothes and almost went into shock, but as I removed my jacket and vest, I realized that it was not my blood and the bulletproof vest had saved me. Thank God for my bulletproof vest! It saved my life that night, I'm sure of it. I looked down to remove the rest of my clothes and saw blood gushing out of my right lower leg where I had been hit. After realizing I was shot in two places, instead of going to the hospital or calling for help, I started getting high on the cocaine that I stashed at my place, to numb the pain. Here comes the crazy part… On that same night, I went to the after-hours club to try to erase from my mind, the episode that had just taken place. I didn't answer my beeper that was blowing up from the crew. I wanted to remove it from my mind. So, I stayed in after-hours spots for days, hustling, drinking champagne, playing with the females, and getting high to escape reality. Enough said.

In the drug world, anything can happen at any time. In the hustle world, one of the street codes is – never trust females. Case in point – we used a lot of females to set up a lot of guys from all walks of life. To acquire our status, we had a certain level of clientele. We did business with almost every profession that you can think of, including doctors, lawyers, judges, pilots, brokers, educators, and business owners. One could not imagine the cash flow that came our way…fast money. Remember, fast money spends fast because it's not valued like hard-earned money. The miracle is that I'm alive to tell this story about a dark part of my life when I was known as the Prince of Darkness.

(Episode 3)

It was a dark and cold night in New York at about 10:45 p.m. on Christmas Eve. I was driving over to my girlfriend's house to take Christmas gifts to her two children. The back seat of my car was full of wrapped gifts. I always took the back roads to get to her house and was about halfway there, when suddenly, I heard sirens and saw police lights flashing in my rearview mirror. I pulled over to the side of the road and two cops got out of the police car. Both cops walked towards my car with their hands on their guns, one on each side of my vehicle. The cop on my side asked for my license and registration and I said, "Sure, officer." As I checked for my documents, I realized that I did not have my wallet and at that moment, all kinds of thoughts ran through my head. I feared going back to jail on a parole violation.

It was very dark in this area and both cops were young white men. I was a Black man alone in a BMW; tall, dark, and handsome, and in tip-top shape. I could tell they were more nervous than I was. I kept telling myself to "stay cool, Prince, and let the situation play out." I'll call them Officer 1 and Officer 2. Officer 1, who came to the driver's side of my car, ordered me to turn off the car and get out when I told him I didn't have the documents. He told me to put my hands on top of the car, and he searched me up and down while Officer 2 pointed his gun at me. Now, remember, I was on a dark back street in New York and it was about 11:30 at night. And when you get stopped without your license and registration in New York, the cops take their sweet time. Officer 1 asked me for my full name and I told him, Prince Blair. Both officers laughed at me because all they heard was Prince, and he asked again in a stronger tone, "What is your real name?" and I repeated myself. At this point, Officer 2 began to search my vehicle, front and back, and would you believe he asked me what was in the gift-wrapped boxes in the back seat? They were obviously Christmas gifts. I almost laughed but the situation was getting tenser by the minute. After searching the inside of my car and not finding anything, they switched, and then Officer 1 searched my car again and still found nothing. While they continued to search my vehicle, another police car pulled up on the scene with two Black officers. I must say I was very nervous when they rolled up. I noticed that these two Black officers were much older than the two white rookie officers who were handling me. One of the officers went over to their car and they exchanged words. The Black officers stayed briefly and then left the scene.

Again, all the attention was back on me. It was now about midnight. Officer 1 asked, "What's in the trunk, Mr. Prince?" laughing at my name and taking the keys to open the trunk. He looked around the trunk and reached in and took out a black, small man's bag. Are you ready for this? Listen closely to what happened next. The officer handed me the black bag and asked, "What's in the bag?" As soon as he passed me the bag, I realized that inside that black bag there was a 9-millimeter Glock, fully loaded and ready to fire. Wow, I could not believe that this rookie police officer had just handed me a fully loaded gun. You could feel the weight of the gun in the bag, and this rookie mistake could have cost him his life. However, someone was praying for me, even then. When I put my hand inside the bag, the first thing I touched was the gun. I put my finger on the trigger and the gun was pointing point-blank at the officer's chest. Like a light switch, my mind quickly clicked into gangster mode and adrenaline took over. I figured I could shoot my way out of the situation. I was sick in my mind, but the thought came into my head and my heart was racing 500 miles per second. The officer was within three feet of me. Then what happened, Prince? I took my hand off the trigger of the gun in this small black bag and surprisingly, felt my wallet that had my license and registration in it. I quickly took the wallet out and handed it to the officer saying, "Here is my wallet with my license and registration in it, Mr. Police Officer, sir," with a big smile on my face, knowing that all my documents were up to date and accurate.

There is more to the story. Listen up. Remember that I told you that both officers searched my vehicle several times? Well, under the driver's side seat mat was 125 grams of compressed cocaine and they missed it. I even forgot that it was there. This happens when you are deep in the dark underworld. When the officer ran my documents, everything checked out clear and they left. I was so relieved, and the tension of the situation was released. When I finally got to my girlfriend's house, she was mad and angry with me because I took so long to get there. All I could do was hold her and say, "If you only knew what I just went through." It was around 1:00 a.m. on Christmas morning, Jesus' birthday. I could go on and on with episode after episode for many dark years of my life. Even now as I write this story about some of my dark past, it seems surreal. Prince of Darkness.

PRINCE THE CHOSEN ONE

Everyone in my crew was dead and I was the only one left. Most people don't know what it feels like when their friends are violently killed. Their deaths haunt you and you have dreams and nightmares about them. I experienced so many of those nightmares in my past that I was at the point where I did not want to go to sleep. For most of the tragedies that occurred, I was supposed to be there, but why wasn't I there? Was I the chosen one?

One night while I was sleeping, I thought, "Here we go again." I asked myself, "Who died this time?" In my dream, I was at another funeral but this one was different. I vividly saw my mother and sisters crying and screaming. As I entered the funeral parlor, I hesitated to walk to the casket. Remembering, I walked very slowly, not wanting to see another one of my homeboys laying in the casket. It seemed like time stood still. When I got to the casket to see the body, everything became blurry. As my vision slowly cleared, I looked down and saw MYSELF in the casket. That explained why I saw my immediate family in my dream. I remember waking up from a deep sleep, screaming out loud, my heart racing, and sweating profusely. It was the scariest moment I've ever experienced in my life. I lived alone and nobody was there but me in my dark bedroom. I kept asking myself, "Are you alive, Prince?" As I laid there, I eventually fell back to sleep and entered back into the same dream. It is very hard to explain this in words but it's true. After wrestling, crying, and fighting through the night, I heard a voice.

It was noticeably clear, saying, "This is your final warning. STOP NOW or it won't be a dream next time." The voice clearly said, "I'm calling you out of darkness into light. Choose now, life or death." The reason I know God is real is that there were four of us in the crew and all of them died violently. I was the worst of the worst and I wondered why I was still the only one alive. That very night God called me out of the world of darkness in which I was comfortable, to serve him with the same passion that I lusted after in the world. First, I had to purge all the things I had accumulated from my dark past, and believe me, I would be lying if I said it was easy. I was very materialistic so little by little I gave away my clothes, sneakers, jewelry, and everything associated with that life. I sold my red customized BMW for almost nothing. None of this was easy but I feared the wrath of God. No one could tell me that God (Jesus) did not have a special plan for my life. I ran to the Lord and didn't look back. That was about 30 years ago.

PRINCE OF PEACE

I remember being at a low point in my life and a friend of mine invited me to go to church with him. Believe me, the church was the last thing on my mind. I was nervous about going but I went anyway. I was nervous because I had not been to church in years. The name of the church was the Greater Allen Cathedral in Queens, New York. Upon entering the main sanctuary of the church, I felt a weird feeling that's hard to explain in words. I felt a cool, comfortable breeze that was refreshing, renewing, and reviving. You see, I was the type of man that didn't smile often; always serious about everything. Many people told me that I was too serious. Strangely enough, I took that as a compliment. My thinking was that life is serious and we need to take it seriously. I thought that men who joked and laughed all the time were clowns. As I looked around this very big church, I saw men, women, and children smiling, laughing, and singing together. I asked myself, "Why are all of these people so happy?" It was like I was in a different world and it was blowing my mind. Suddenly, everyone got quiet and the preacher started teaching and preaching the word of God. Now I was really lost because I couldn't keep up nor did I understand what he was talking about. But it did feel good to listen to strong, powerful words being spoken and to watch the people react to what he was saying. Wow! The only thing that upset me that day was when church was over. In church, I felt like a child at his first visit to Disney World. I couldn't remember feeling that good in a long time. Although my friend who invited me stopped going to church, I still went on my own. I joined the church and became dedicated and fully committed.

I was at church every time the doors were open, and my family began to call me a Jesus addict. My whole life was to please God for letting me live. After several years serving in the church, I met my lovely wife Michelle. I wasn't looking for a wife at the time. I was married to Jesus and I was satisfied. During the church offering, the entire congregation would walk around the church to place their tithes and offerings into the baskets. I noticed Michelle and she was beautiful, elegant, and had the prettiest smile I had ever seen. It seemed like sunshine beamed through her. It was like a bright sunny day every time I saw her. I thought to myself, "I know she is married, and her husband is a lucky man." Real talk. When the service started, I forgot all about her and focused my attention on the preached word.

One Sunday morning before service began, as she walked towards the entrance of the church, our eyes met, and she had that beautiful smile again. We briefly talked and laughed together, and she went inside. The Allen Cathedral is a megachurch and I always sat front and center to be close to the altar, and as I walked to my seat, as faith would have it, Michelle was sitting there right next to where I had left my briefcase. We worshiped together on that Sunday morning and it was as if God placed her there for me. We nurtured our relationship, and I knew she was the one. As they say, the rest is history. We have been happily married for 20 years and counting. God answers prayer.

PRINCE THE CHAMPION

Like a prodigal son, I returned to the foundation I was taught early in my life. I was once lost in a world of darkness but now I walk in the world of God's light. Not knowing then what I know now, in all the episodes that should have killed me, God spared me. What the enemy meant for evil, God turned around for my good. Through all my trials in life, I've learned that after the lesson comes the blessing. God had a plan for me even then. Although I never knew my biological father, I always had a heavenly father that was protecting me and keeping me. The hardest part of writing my story was revealing things that I was always fearful of sharing, but now it brings me a feeling of liberation and freedom. Many people will judge us on our past, but I am so glad that man does not have the power to judge me. Only God is my judge. I now share parts of my past experiences to help others see the light of God in their own lives.

My life has transformed from a world of darkness to that of marvelous light. I am the proud father of two incredible children whom I love with all my heart. My daughter Destiny is a beautiful young lady. She has a caring spirit and is very independent. She has given me my first grandson, Damon, who is special in my life. My son Prince Jr. is a gift from God. He is talented, smart, and kind-hearted. He's my sidekick and I take joy in raising him to be all that God intends for him to be. As a husband, I am blessed. The Bible says in Proverbs 18:22 when a man finds a wife, he finds a good thing and obtains favor from the Lord. God has given me my wife Michelle whom I love and adore. I am so grateful for my family. I am currently a licensed and ordained minister under the anointed pastor, T.J. McBride of Tabernacle of Praise Church International where our vision is to reach lost souls for Jesus Christ, that all men may be saved, by any means necessary.

The true definition of a champion is to never give up. As I look back on my past, I recognize the champion within me. Although my life has had its ups and downs, through perseverance, my mother's prayers, inner strength, lessons learned, forgiveness, love, and support, and most importantly, God's hand over my life, I still rose as a CHAMPION. The Bible says, "Train up a child in the way he should go and when he is old, he will not depart from it." (Proverbs 22:6) I am grateful for a praying mother and because of the foundation of God she instilled in me as a child, I returned to my first love. God is love.

ABOUT
PRINCE BLAIR

Prince Blair is a minister, motivational speaker, teacher, mentor, and leader of men.

He was born and raised in Queens, New York, in a single-parent household. This prodigal son grew up in the Baptist Church and knew God early in his childhood. As time passed, this Christian foundation proved to manifest itself later in his life. Succumbing to the forces of his environment, his life began to take a downward spiral into darkness. However, by the grace of God, he rose to become a champion.

Prince holds a bachelor's degree from ITT Technical Institute and has worked in the technology field for over 30 years. He has always been an analytical and forward thinker. However, his passion is to save boys from self-destruction by teaching them their identity, possibilities, and responsibilities, as they grow into manhood. Prince has taken gang members, drug dealers, and lost boys off the street corners in some of the worst neighborhoods of New York. Their future seemed dim but through his guidance, he was able to witness change for so many, including self-respect and a positive attitude. Many have gone on to become high school and college graduates who got jobs and turned their life around for the better. To God be the glory!

As a dedicated member of The Greater Allen Cathedral in Queens, New York, with over 25,000 members, Prince was assigned as the Director to lead the young men mentoring program called Rites of Passage. He has also led the men's ministry, prison ministry, and served as an associate to his pastor. In New York, Prince attended Nyack Seminary College and received a Certificate of Theology. Upon relocating with his family to Georgia, God led him to Tabernacle of Praise Church International and he answered his call to ministry. He is a licensed and ordained minister in New York and Georgia.

Prince has been married for 20 years and counting to his lovely wife Michelle, whom he affectionately calls "Glorious." His two children, Destiny and Prince Jr., are his motivation and he is the proud grandfather of Damon.

Prince believes that there is a champion in every man, and he is committed to helping them discover the champion within.

Made in the USA
Columbia, SC
09 February 2021